MW01285080

Teaching Children Self-Control

Give children the skills and strategies they need to control their impulses!

Jamie Goldring

Illustrations

By

Amy Hutcheson & Evan Cooper

Book Design

By

Heather Farmer Crutcher

ISBN: 9781480229648

Also by Jamie Goldring

Discover ME
I Believe
Tools and Techniques For Teaching Children Self-Control

Ms. Goldring earned her B.A. in Sociology from California State University and her M.A. in Speech Pathology from the University of Memphis.

Contents

Introduction

Sound familiar? *Pay attention, stop pushing, don't hit, stop screaming, share, don't interrupt, turn it down, I said no, I can't understand you when you are crying, calm down, stop grabbing, be quiet, it's not your turn, don't touch, don't yell at me, look at me when I'm talking to you, get control of yourself!*

It seems as though we are always asking our children to learn and behave, but are we effectively teaching them how?

Children who learn self-control at a young age are better prepared to deal with their emotions. Competency in self-control lays the groundwork for children to deal with more complex situations later in life.

As children get older the behaviors become more challenging and you will hear yourself constantly chanting these familiar words. *Clean your room, do your homework, don't talk back to me, drop the attitude, I said no, you have a curfew, don't raise your voice to me, don't drink and drive, don't talk on the phone and drive, don't text and drive, don't do drugs, don't have sex, don't have unprotected sex!* These behaviors all require self-control and self-regulation.

This program is designed to give children the skills and strategies they need to control their impulses. It is designed to create self-awareness, emotional competence, and mindfulness — developing and strengthening the connection between the body and mind.

What are Executive Functions?

The executive functions of the brain are housed in the prefrontal areas of the frontal lobe. These skills include:

- Self-Control (impulse-control)/Self-Regulation
- Focus/Attention/Concentration
- Planning/Organization
- Memory
- Abstract Thinking/Reasoning
- Problem-Solving

Research has revealed that giving children the opportunity to practice these critical skills can strengthen these cognitive processes. Research tells us that self-control is essential for academic success and necessary for making good judgments and choices. Research has also revealed that self-control plays a more significant role towards academic achievement than a high IQ.

The activities in this book are designed to teach children the skills they need to control their impulses. Research has revealed that teaching these skills improves behavior and academic performance.

Activities are designed to strengthen these cognitive abilities by practicing these critical skills. These cognitive processes play an important role in our everyday lives.

How to Teach Self-Control

If you are a parent or teacher the first skill you should teach your children is self-control. Self-control plays a significant role in learning and in life.

- Self-control is a learned skill just as math, English, reading, and writing are learned.
- We are not born with the skills we need to read, write, do math, or use self-control. We are taught these skills.
- We need to teach children self-control just as we need to teach children how to read, write, or do math.
- If you want children to learn math, teach them the skills and strategies they need to add and subtract.
- If you want children to learn self-control, teach children the skills and strategies they need to control their impulses.

So why are schools and parents not teaching self-control when we know how important it is for the future success of our children? Why do we not have a self-control curriculum like we have a reading or a math curriculum?

Self-control should be taught to children like any other subject! Parents and teachers need to understand self-control to teach self-control just as they need to understand math to teach math.

How do we teach math?

- Break it down into various concepts and skills, such as number recognition, counting, adding, subtracting, and multiplying.
- Why do we give math homework and classroom activities? To give children the opportunity to practice adding, subtracting, multiplying, etc.
- The more opportunities children are given to practice math, the more competent they become with these skills.
- We need to give children the tools and strategies they need to become competent in math.

How do we teach self-control? The same way we teach math or reading.

- Break self-control down into various concepts and skills.
- Plan activities to give children the opportunity to practice self-control at home and in the classroom.
- The more opportunities children are given to practice self-control, the more competent they become with the skills and strategies they need to control the things they say and do.
- Practice encourages competence!
- It is the responsibility of parents and teachers to prepare children to become competent with these skills that encourage self-control. Give children the tools and strategies they need to control their behavior in a positive way!

So how do we teach these critical skills, such as self-control and focus, that research has repeatedly confirmed to be essential for academic success and necessary for making good judgments and choices? First we need to understand self-control.

What is Self-Control?

- Self-control is the ability to control your own behavior in a positive way and — to stop and think before you act.
- It is understanding the positive and negative consequences for what you choose to say and do and — taking responsibility for your thoughts and actions.
- It is Mental/Emotional Strength – The ability to use your mental strength to control your body — being strong enough mentally to encourage your body to respond to your emotions in a positive way (mind-body connection) and — understanding your feelings/emotions.
- Self-control is being in charge of your thoughts and your body.
- Self-control encourages the development of one's internal strength to listen attentively (to yourself as well as others) while ignoring distractions.
- Self-control is learned!

We learn self-control by creating and developing positive thoughts. Sometimes without thinking our bodies simply react in a negative way to various situations. Our positive thoughts give us the tools and strategies we need to say to ourselves *"stop and think"* or *"calm down."* Children need to learn that they are capable of controlling their impulses.

It's important to teach children how to create and use positive thoughts to control their bodies and — the way their bodies respond to their emotions.

When we are engaged in self-control — what are we actually controlling? We are controlling our thoughts and we use our thoughts to control our bodies. Self-control enhances the connection between the body and mind.

When children gain experience controlling their thoughts and actions by responding to their emotions in a positive way, they begin to understand that they have the ability to control themselves and their lives. This encourages self-confidence!

Children need to practice moving their bodies in different ways and practice calming their bodies down. Practicing the techniques and strategies needed to stop and think before you act encourages competence in self-control and self-regulation. This gives children the confidence they need to effectively implement these essential skills into their daily lives.

The Recipe for Self-Control

- Competent Language Skills
- Positive Behavior
- Body Awareness
- Focus/Concentration
- Mental/Emotional Strength
- Confidence
- Patience
- Listening
- Respect
- Empathy
- Practice

Curriculums should include activities that give children the opportunity to learn, develop, and practice self-control and self-regulation.

Provide an activity each day to give children the opportunity to practice the ingredients that make up the recipe for self-control. The more they practice these skills, the more competent they become at controlling their impulses.

Self-Control Begins by Teaching:

(1) Competent Language Skills:

- Teach children the language and vocabulary they need to understand their feelings and to express their emotions in a positive way.
- Children need to be taught how to recognize, understand, identify, and explain their feelings.
- Encourage children to discuss their emotions by explaining and describing their feelings for them, for example, *I can see you are feeling frustrated. You are squeezing your hands and clenching your teeth together. Sometimes you can even feel your heart beating fast. I see when you get angry you feel like screaming, hitting,* or *throwing something.* Teach children positive ways to handle their emotions. *Let's think of some different ways we can calm our bodies down and let go of the anger.*
- Teach children how to communicate with themselves and others. Children learn to communicate with themselves through self-talk. Self-talk is repeating positive statements to yourself to build mental and emotional strength, such as, *I am the boss of my own body, I am strong enough to deal with this situation,* or *I am smart!* This encourages a positive self-image and a high self-esteem, which inspires confidence. Self-talk also encourages emotional and body awareness.
- Teach children to use their emotional/mental strength to encourage their bodies to listen to their positive thoughts to implement appropriate behavior.
- Encourage children to use their positive thoughts to control their impulses.
- Organization & Planning – Teach children to organize their thoughts and actions to effectively communicate and carry out their ideas, complete tasks, and accomplish goals. Effectively coordinating your thoughts and actions encourages abstract thinking, problem solving, and reasoning skills.

- Visualization/Guided Imagery – Encourage children to use visualization to calm their bodies by creating mental images of their positive thoughts and ideas. It's important that these invisible concepts become visible to children.

(2) Positive Behavior:

- Teach children appropriate ways to act in various social settings.
- Encourage children to recognize and understand what their bodies are doing and how their bodies are acting in different situations, for example, in the car, at mealtime, at the movies, in church or synagogue, at the library, when someone is sleeping, at someone else's house, in school, on the playground, or when they are feeling mad, angry, or frustrated.
- Personal Space – Understanding where your body is in space and how it relates to others.

(3) Body Awareness:

- Through body awareness children begin to understand their bodies, what their bodies are capable of, and that they are responsible for their bodies.
- Through body awareness children begin to understand the importance of being mentally and emotionally in control of yourself (your thoughts and your actions) and that YOU are responsible for the things you choose to say and do.
- Children need to be aware of the way their bodies feel and change when they are experiencing various feelings and emotions. For example, encourage children to use their words to explain how their bodies feel when they are angry, happy, or sad. Children need to be aware of the way their bodies feel and know how to control their actions. Teach children positive ways to deal with their many different feelings.
- Mind-Body Coordination – Encourage the development of mental, emotional, and physical awareness. Give children the opportunity to effectively coordinate their thoughts and actions (mind-body connection) to accomplish their goals. Provide exercises and activities for children that build mental and emotional strength to control their bodies (actions) in a positive way. Your feelings and emotions are connected to your body and affect the way your body responds. Motor planning, sequencing, and breathing activities increase body awareness and encourage mind-body coordination.
- Breathe/Relax – Children need to practice breathing and relaxing their bodies. Encourage children to take breaks throughout the day to acknowledge the way their bodies feel. Take a body break! Stop, recognize and identify your feelings, breathe, and relax. Teach children the strategies and techniques they need to mentally and emotionally calm their bodies to control their actions.

(4) Focus & Concentration:

- Provide activities to encourage and strengthen mental attention.
- Encourage children to pay attention to themselves, others, and their surroundings.
- Give children the opportunity to think, pay attention, and focus on things they cannot see.

(5) Mental/Emotional Strength:

- Using positive thoughts (brainpower) to control one's body to build internal strength.
- This gives children the opportunity to see themselves as strong confident individuals who have the ability to control and manage their own behavior.
- This strength and confidence in yourself builds a positive self-image and encourages a high self-esteem.

(6) Confidence:

- Believing in yourself — knowing that you have the necessary skills to approach life's challenges with the strength, courage, and power to control your body and your thoughts.
- Trusting yourself to effectively manage your own behavior in positive ways.

(7) Patience:

- Delayed gratification versus immediate gratification.
- Learning to wait.

(8) Listening:

- Not just hearing the words, but listening to the words to remember and understand the information.
- Listening includes focusing on the person who is talking and on the words you are hearing, maintaining eye contact, and not interrupting.
- Learning to listen to yourself as well as others.

(9) Respect:

- Being kind and thoughtful to others.

(10)   Empathy:

- Understanding the feelings of others.

(11)   Practice:

- Practice encourages competence! Competence encourages confidence!

Teach children the skills and strategies they need to calm their thoughts and their bodies before a situation occurs. Teach these skills when children are calm and relaxed.

Once these strategies have been taught give children the opportunity to practice these skills when they are calm. Children need to be prepared so they can respond in a positive way to their many different feelings.

The more opportunities children are given to practice, the more competent they become with the skills they need to control their impulses and — incorporate these skills into their everyday lives.

The ultimate goal is to encourage children to:

- Manage their own behavior.
- Take responsibility for their actions.
- Stop and think about the consequences for what they choose to say and do.
- Make positive choices.
- Resolve conflicts peacefully.

Remember, self-control is learned just like you learn to read, write, or do math. It takes time to develop self-control and lots of practice to use it effectively to control your behavior.

Competency in the skills and strategies needed to handle life's many challenges encourages self-confidence. Confidence encourages children to trust and believe in themselves!

Suggestions for Calming Your Thoughts and Your Body

(1) Teach children a positive phrase to say to themselves (self-talk). For example, say to yourself: *I am in charge of my own body, relax and stay calm, I'm strong enough to keep my hands in my lap, or I can do this if I keep trying!* Encourage them to use these positive thoughts to get control of their bodies.

(2) Encourage children to talk about their feelings with a teacher, parent, or friend.

(3) Take a body break. For example, walk away and take charge of your actions or tell yourself to stop your body and calm down.

(4) Ask yourself, *if I do this, what could happen?* Encourage children to stop and think about the positive and negative consequences for what they choose to say and do.

(5) Breathe/relax. Give your body the opportunity to calm down. Be patient and communicate with yourself.

(6) Sit in your **Quiet & Still** (p.36) or **Peace** pose (p.71).

(7) Listen to quiet and peaceful music.

(8) Visualization/guided imagery. Visualize yourself doing something that is calming or something that makes you feel good about yourself, such as, playing with your dog, dancing, lying on the beach, helping a friend, etc.

(9) Focus/concentration. Focus and concentrate on your positive thoughts and your body. For example, *when I say the words kindness and caring to myself it reminds me to think about the way others feel.*

(10) Easy/soft stretches. *My body feels calm and relaxed when I gently stretch.*

(11) Positive physical release, such as, jogging, dancing, or playing basketball.

(12) Keep a calm down box in your child's room or in your classroom. Fill this box with different things for children to use to calm their bodies, thoughts, and actions. Encourage responsibility by letting the children help choose the different items to keep in their boxes. The following list includes suggestions of different things you may want to keep in your calm down box.

- Glitter Jar – (p.61)
- STAR (picture) – (p.127)
- Breathing (maraca, bells) – (p.136)
- Quiet & Still/Peace Pose (pictures) – (pp.36 & 71))
- Empathy Stone or Velvet Fabric – (pp.94 &101)
- Sponges or Squeeze Balls
- Stuffed Animal
- CD player and CD's (peaceful music)
- Paper and Crayons
- Self-Talk (positive messages kept in a small box that your child has written). These messages serve as reminders to help children feel good about themselves and remember what they are supposed to do to take control of their bodies. For example, *I am strong enough to not interrupt while others are talking* or *I am smart.* A parent or teacher may help write these positive messages (or thoughts) to help their children calm their bodies when they hear them (p.80). Pictures can also be used to illustrate positive thoughts, such as, a happy face or a child's pet.

(13) Plan ahead. Discuss with your children which strategies and techniques they plan to use to calm their bodies and take control of their actions.

(14) Be prepared! Practice with your children (when they are calm) the strategies and techniques they plan to use to take control of their thoughts and actions before a situation occurs. Practice encourages competence. Competence encourages confidence — believing in yourself!

Positive Language Encourages Positive Behavior

Positive language states to your child *"what you should do" and "what is expected"* in a meaningful, caring, and constructive way.

Instead of Saying:

- *Don't throw the ball in the house* **Say** *if you want to play with the ball please go outside.*
- *Stop screaming in the hallway* **Say** *please talk quietly in the hallway.*
- *Don't tear the pages in the book* **Say** *books are for reading.*
- *Don't leave your toys on the floor* **Say** *when you are finished playing please put your toys back in the closet.*
- *Don't eat that cake before dinner* **Say** *after you have finished eating you can have dessert.*
- *Stop all the noise* **Say** *I need you to use quiet voices so I can concentrate on my work.*
- *Don't break in line* **Say** *please go to the end of the line and wait for your turn.*
- *Don't grab that puzzle* **Say** *when she is finished with the puzzle then you can play with it.*
- *You can't ride your bike* **Say** *when you have finished your homework you can ride your bike.*
- *Don't make a mess in the room* **Say** *when you are finished please put everything back where you got it.*
- *Don't take my book* **Say** *just ask me if you would like to borrow my book.*
- *Don't come inside with muddy shoes* **Say** *please leave your shoes outside if they are muddy.*
- *Don't wipe your hands on your clothes* **Say** *if your hands are dirty please use your napkin.*
- *Don't stomp your feet* **Say** *if you are feeling angry, breathe and tell your feet to calm down and relax.*
- *Don't squeeze his hands* **Say** *when standing in the circle gently hold your partner's hands.*
- *Stop crying, he didn't mean to break your truck* **Say** *I know you are feeling angry and upset because he broke your truck. Let's see if we can fix it.*
- *Stop whining and crying* **Say** *when you have stopped crying and are ready to talk I'll be in the kitchen.*

To encourage communication between children, teacher and child, or parent and child, ask the following questions to encourage and reinforce positive behavior.

Children need to learn how to verbalize their feelings by stating what they did, why they did it, and what they are going to do about it. When you verbalize your feelings it creates emotional, mental, and body awareness.

The questions on the following pages encourage children to understand and become aware of their feelings and the feelings of others. It encourages children to take responsibility for the things they choose to say and do.

When talking to children always establish eye contact and frequently use their names. This personalizes the relationship and encourages children to stay focused and concentrate on the spoken words.

Choose to ask as many questions as you feel are appropriate depending on the situation and the age of the children, such as, instead of saying, *"don't push!"* and punishing the child, the teacher engages the children in the following dialogue.

Example #1: The teacher asks:

Susie, what happened (or what is the problem)? John pushed me down.
John, what are you doing? Pushing.
John, why are you pushing? Because I want to go first.
John, why should you not push? Pushing can hurt someone. Pushing is a bad choice. We use our hands to help people.
John, how do you feel when someone pushes you? Sad. Why? Because it hurts.
John, what should you do instead of pushing (or let's think of some other things we can say or do instead of pushing)? Get control of my body. Calm my body down. Wait my turn.
John, how do you plan to calm your body down? Breathe and relax. Say to myself, stop my body and calm down. Sit in my **Quiet & Still** pose.
John, what are you supposed to be doing? Waiting calmly for my turn.
John, how are you supposed to be sitting? With my legs crisscrossed and my hands in my lap.
John, lets practice together what you are going to do to control your actions when you are feeling angry.

Once John and the teacher have determined the positive behavior that John is supposed to do instead of pushing, which is to calm his thoughts and his body by sitting in the **Quiet and Still** pose, give John the opportunity to practice this behavior every day.

Role-playing is also an effective method that can be used to encourage positive behavior. Set up a situation with the child and pretend to push and shove. Ask, *what are you going to do when someone pushes you? How can you get your self-control when you are mad and feel like pushing? Let's practice together sitting in the **Quiet and Still** pose and breathe.*

Puppet shows can also be effective. This gives children the opportunity to see others using positive behaviors to resolve conflicts peacefully. It also stimulates discussion about one's feelings and emotions.

Create skills that are challenging for children to learn. Provide a skill that is difficult to achieve the first time it is attempted, but easy enough to be mastered with continued practice. This teaches children that it takes time and practice to learn a new skill. You don't always accomplish something the first time you try and that it's ok to make a mistake.

Encourage children to confront challenging situations by verbalizing their feelings to themselves and others and — teaching them how to control their actions.

Example #2: Dialogue between children with parent or teacher guidance:

John: Sam, stop being so bossy!
Teacher: Sam, what does John want you to stop doing?
Sam: To stop being so bossy.
Teacher: John tell Sam what you want him to stop doing?
John: Stop bossing me around and telling me what to do!
Teacher: What do you think both of you could do to get along with each other?
John: Take turns.
Sam: We each get to decide what to do when it's our turn.
Teacher: John, tell Sam if you agree to take turns to decide what to do.
Teacher: Sam, tell John if that's ok with you to take turns.
Teacher: So everyone agrees to take turns. Both of you came up with a good solution to this problem. No one has to be bossy. You each get to decide what to do when it's your turn.

Give children the opportunity to participate in the "solution process." Always ask the children involved in the conflict, *let's think of some different ways we can handle this situation that works for both of you. Let's stop and think before you decide what to do.*

Giving children the opportunity to express their needs creates emotional awareness in themselves and others. This strategy prepares children to handle conflicts peacefully by letting them experience and participate in the "solution process." This method inspires confidence in yourself to handle challenging situations.

This is empowering for children when they realize that they have control over their own lives by the choices they make. Children begin to understand that their choices affect the outcome of a situation.

Remember to acknowledge children's behavior for making positive choices. Describe what they are doing with the appropriate language to give them the opportunity to recognize and identify their feelings and the feelings of others.

Example #3:

Teacher: Sarah, what are you doing?
Sarah: Sharing my book with Laura.
Teacher: Sarah, why are you sharing your book with Laura?
Sarah: Because she wants to look at it too.
Teacher: Laura, how do you feel when Sarah shares her books with you?
Laura: Happy.

Children need to understand that there are positive and negative consequences for their actions. For example, ask yourself, *if I do this, what could happen? If I choose to share my book with Laura, we could have fun playing together and become friends (positive consequences). If I choose not to share my book with Laura, she will be mad and won't play with me (negative consequences).*

It's important that children understand that their choices and actions can result in either a positive or a negative outcome. You are in charge of the things you say and do! Teach children to stop and think about the consequences, both positive and negative, for what they choose to say and do.

Children experience many different feelings throughout the day. They need to understand that it's ok to feel angry, upset, frustrated, sad, happy, excited, scared, etc. Teach children the skills, strategies, language, and vocabulary they need to express their feelings and deal with their emotions in a positive way.

This question and answer dialogue inspires empathy. Children need to understand that their actions affect the feelings of others. Repeat this quote to yourself, *"It matters to me how others feel."* Encourage children to understand the true meaning of this message.

Communicate with your child! Stimulate language and conversation by reading, talking, and asking children open-ended questions, such as, what, why, when, where, and how.

Tips for Parents and Teachers

(1)   Communicate and connect with your children by participating in the activities with them.

(2)   Be a positive role model. Children imitate behavior. Children need to see their parents and teachers express their feelings and respond to them in a positive way (using self-control). This teaches children appropriate ways to handle and express their many different emotions. Children need to see others using positive behaviors to resolve conflicts peacefully.

(3)   Teach children how to communicate effectively. Children need a feelings vocabulary to communicate their needs verbally. They need to identify, label, and understand their feelings.

(4)   Body awareness. Encourage children to be aware of the physical changes in their bodies when they experience different emotions, such as, the way their bodies feel when they are upset versus the way their bodies feel when they are calm.

(5)   Empathy. Teach children to identify, label, and understand the feelings of others.

(6)   Teach self-control. Give children the skills and strategies they need to control their impulses: their bodies, their thoughts, and their actions. Practice these skills and strategies when they are calm and relaxed.

(7)   Problem-solving. Encourage your child to stop and think of different ways to handle various situations.

(8)   Children need to have an understanding of consequences. They need to stop and think about the consequences, both positive and negative, for what they choose to say and do. Remind children to ask themselves, *if I choose to do this, what could happen?*

(9)   Practice with your child the positive behavior he or she should do instead of the negative behavior.

(10)   Be a good listener. Stop what you are doing, focus on your child, and pay attention to what is being said.

(11)   Teach listening skills. Play games that encourage effective listening.

(12)   Teach focus. Play games that encourage eye contact and concentration.

(13)   Be observant. Pay close attention to your child's behavior. Acknowledge your child for using self-control and making positive choices such as, saying to your child, *thank-you for waiting. That took a lot of patience to not interrupt me while I was talking on the phone. You have self-control. Or it takes strength and power to wait for your turn. You can control the way you act.* Use appropriate language to describe children's actions to encourage these positive behaviors.

(14)   Describe your child's behavior, such as, *that took self-control to make yourself whisper and move quietly while the others were sleeping. You should feel proud of yourself. No one had to tell you what to do or how to act. Or I noticed your friend was getting upset trying to ride her bike. You were so kind to help her. That took patience.* "Good choices" encourage positive consequences. Cooperation and getting along with others inspires positive relationships.

(15)   Role-playing. Set up pretend situations and give children the opportunity to act out their feelings and practice using positive ways to handle their emotions.

(16)   Use reminders. For example, set a timer for 10 minutes. Tell your child, *when the bell rings that means it's time to stop coloring and brush your teeth.* Ask your child, *what are you going to do when you hear the bell?* Your child should repeat what he or she is supposed to do to ensure he understands the directions. Talk to your child by asking questions such as, *why do you need to brush your teeth* (positive consequences)? *What would happen to your teeth if you didn't brush them* (negative consequences)?

(17) Triggers. Plan ahead! Be aware of different things that trigger both positive and negative behaviors. For example, every time another child plays with your child's truck you notice he or she gets upset or your child becomes frustrated when trying to finish a puzzle. Prepare children by giving them plenty of opportunities to practice these strategies to encourage positive behavior (actions).

(18) Ask your child to join you in practicing the **Quiet & Still** pose (p.36) or the **Peace** pose (p.71). Practicing these poses allows you the time you need to stop your body and think about the way your body feels. Let your child see you take a body break to calm down, relax, and get control of your thoughts and actions. It's important that children see their parents and teachers practice the same methods they are teaching them.

(19) Talk and read to your child. Include books that encourage positive behavior in various social settings and books that explain feelings, emotions, and stimulate language.

(20) Give children specific chores at home and in the classroom to encourage responsibility. This gives children the opportunity to feel good about themselves for their accomplishments.

(21) Encourage children to be proud of themselves for good judgment and positive choices based on their conscience, not a reward, such as *that took self-control and confidence to stand up for yourself and your friend in front of everyone.*

(22) Be consistent. Say what you mean and mean what you say!

Remember, practice self-control with your child when he or she is calm. The more opportunities children are given to practice these skills that encourage self-control, the more competent they become in using these techniques to control and manage their own behavior. The key to self-control is practice, practice, practice! Practice encourages competence! Competence encourages confidence!

The Peace Code

This code, created to promote peace and self-control, should be implemented by parents, teachers, and anyone involved with children!

- **P** is for Practice the Power. Empower children with the skills and strategies they need to manage and control their own behavior in a positive way. Practicing these skills encourages competence. Competence encourages confidence – believing in yourself!
- **E** is for Educate and Engage Children Emotionally. Educate yourself by learning the importance of self-control. Practice self-control to build mental and emotional strength to teach yourself and others to manage their own behavior. Interact and engage children daily in social and emotional dialogue (understanding & expressing their feelings).
- **A** is for Advocate. Support and encourage self-control, discipline, and peace at home, in the classroom, and in the community.
- **C** is for Communicate and Connect. Open up the lines of communication and stay connected with your children socially and emotionally.
- **E** is for equal. We are all created equal.

Teach Children the Peace Pledge (p. 74)

I believe in peace.
Peace begins within yourself.
I promise to be kind, thoughtful, and respectful to others.
I believe in peace.
Peace for you and me.
P is for power — the power of peace.
P is for possibilities. I promise to follow my dreams.
P is for perseverance. I promise to never give up.
E is for ethical. I promise to be fair, honest, and good.
A is for advocate. I promise to work hard for peace.
C is for control — self-control. I promise to take responsibility for the things I say and do.
E is for equal. We are all created equal.
I believe in peace.
Peace for you and me!

The Activities and Discussions are Designed to:

- Teach children how to control their impulses by giving them the skills and strategies they need to manage their own behavior.
- Encourage children to build a positive relationship with themselves and others.
- Encourage children to stop and think about the consequences of their behavior.
- Teach children how to apply these critical skills that are essential for making good judgments and choices into their daily lives.
- Teach children how to recognize, identify, and understand their feelings through self-awareness.
- Give children the opportunity to express themselves by communicating with themselves and others.
- Enhance the connection between the body and mind — teaching children how to organize their thoughts and actions in a positive way to resolve conflicts peacefully and accomplish their goals.
- Encourage children through practice and repetition to internalize these abstract concepts, such as, self-control and focus and — teach them how to develop these concepts into meaningful and concrete ideas.
- Build mental and emotional strength to encourage the development of self-control, high self-esteem, confidence and — believing in yourself!

Practicing these essential skills encourage children to automatically respond in a positive way to their feelings. Remember, the key to self-control is practice! Practice encourages competence! Competence encourages confidence!

Summary

Self-control should be your first objective at home and in the classroom! Give children the skills and strategies they need to control their impulses!

Children need to understand and acknowledge their feelings, but learn how to control their actions. Teach children the things they say and do are a choice. You can't control what other people say and do, but you can control the things you say and do — how you choose to deal with life's challenges.

When children gain experience controlling their thoughts and actions by responding to their emotions in a positive way, they begin to understand that they have the ability to control themselves and their lives. This encourages confidence — believing in yourself!

This is empowering for children and adults when they realize that they have control over their own lives by the choices they make, understanding that their choices affect the outcome of a situation.

Self-control is learned and should be taught like any other subject. The ultimate goal is to encourage children to:

- Manage their own behavior.
- Take responsibility for their actions.
- Stop and think about the consequences, both positive and negative, for what they choose to say and do.
- Make positive choices.
- Resolve conflicts peacefully (within yourself and others).

* How to Use This Book

This book was written to provide parents and teachers an easy and effective way to begin teaching self-control.

- After reading pages five through twenty-two, begin with activity #1 (p. 25) and progress in order through activity #52.
- Each activity is divided into exercises.
- Familiarize yourself with each lesson plan before you begin teaching. When explaining the directions put them into your own words.
- Specific skills and strategies are introduced in each activity. Children are given the opportunity to practice these techniques and incorporate these skills into their daily lives.
- The questions and examples included in the activities are suggestions designed to motivate discussion about these important concepts. You may want to create your own questions and examples to accommodate the needs of various age groups.
- End each activity by practicing your breathing in one of the calming poses, such as, the **Peace**, **Relax**, or **Quiet & Still** pose. This gives children the opportunity to connect to their feelings. It increases the understanding that you can create a calm and relaxed body. It encourages peaceful actions.
- Activities are easy to modify to accommodate the developmental needs of various age groups to encourage challenging and successful experiences.
- Activities can be lengthened or shortened so they are easy to incorporate into your curriculum on a daily basis.
- Repeat the activities to give children the opportunity to practice these essential skills that encourage self-control.

The information and activities in this book may be used as a format to create your own ideas, activities, and lesson plans.

Additional activities for teaching self-control can also be found in my books *Discover ME* and *Tools and Techniques for Teaching Children Self-Control*. The activities in these books are designed to encourage children to learn important lifelong skills while having fun!

To learn more about teaching children self-control please visit www.teachingselfcontrol.com or contact jgoldie721@aol.com.

Activities

Activity #1: Introduce Yourself

Materials Needed:

- A colored piece of masking tape.

Directions:

The teacher and the children sit on the floor in a circle in a person-space pattern. A person-space pattern is sitting or standing with a space between your bodies so your bodies are not touching each other.

Place a piece of colored tape in the middle of the circle.

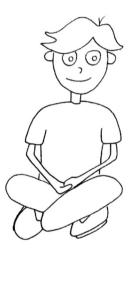

Person-Space Pattern

Exercise #1:

The teacher says, "Let's introduce ourselves." The teacher asks the following questions and tells everyone to shout out the answer at the same time.

- What is your name?
- How old are you?
- What is your favorite color?
- Name something that you love to do.
- What is the name of one of your friends?
- What is your favorite snack?

The teacher says, "I didn't learn anything about you. It's hard to hear, listen, understand, and remember when everyone is shouting and talking at the same time. Let's try introducing ourselves again. This time let's organize how we are going to introduce ourselves so we can hear, listen, understand, and remember."
Discuss with your students different ways to organize this activity.

Suggestions:

- Talk one at a time and use a soft voice. Take turns.
- When waiting for your turn sit quiet and still with your hands in your lap. Look at the person who is talking.
- When it's your turn stand and walk quietly to the piece of colored tape that is placed in the middle of the circle. Stand on the tape and say: my name is………….
- Look at all your friends in the circle when you are talking to them.
- When standing and sitting move your body without a sound.

The teacher goes first and demonstrates what you are supposed to do. For example, the teacher quietly walks over and stands on the piece of colored tape and says, "My name is………" The teacher returns to his or her space. The person next to the teacher goes second, and so on around the circle, until everyone has had a turn.

Repeat this same format giving the teacher and the children the opportunity to tell their friends something about themselves.

Suggestions:

- My name is …………… and I love to ……………
- My name is …………… and my favorite color is ……………
- My name is …………… and I'm happy when I'm ……………
- My name is …………… and I like my friends to ……………
- My name is …………… and this is my friend …………… (the person who is being introduced stands on the piece of colored tape and says hello. A friend can only be introduced once so everyone in the circle has a turn to be introduced).

The teacher asks:

- What happened when we all talked at the same time?
- Why should we take turns?
- Why should you not interrupt when others are talking?
- Why is it important to listen while others are talking?

Exercise #2:

The teacher explains that self-control is:

- Being in charge of your own body.
- It is taking control of your body and telling your body what to do.

The teacher asks, "When you control your body what are you actually controlling? You are controlling your hands, your feet, your voice, your head, your shoulders, your arms, and your thoughts. You are controlling your whole body."

Self-control is being in charge of the things you say and do. Self-control is being able to control your own behavior (your actions).

Directions:

The teacher says, "Show me you can control your body (your hands, feet, voice, etc.) and you are in charge of yourself. We are going to play a game. I'm going to call out different ways for you to control the way your body moves. Move your body with no voices."

The teacher calls out the following directions for the children to demonstrate:

- Sit quietly.
- Control your eyes. Make your eyes look at me.
- Clap your hands. Stop your hands.
- Shake one hand. Make your hand stop.
- Put your hands in your lap.
- Control your shoulders by making them move up and down.
- Slowly make your head move all around.
- Without making a sound, stand up.
- Control your feet. Make your feet march in place.
- Make your feet tiptoe in place.
- Make your feet jog in place.
- Balance on one foot.
- Make your body jump three times and stop your body.
- Lower your body to the floor without a sound.
- Sit quietly.
- Count to ten in a quiet voice (whispering).
- Count to ten in a loud voice.
- Jump up and down while moving your arms slowly all around.
- Make your body stop moving.
- Stand perfectly still while I count to ten.
- Put your hands near your head.
- Place your body on the floor without a sound and sit quietly with your hands in your lap.
- Whisper to yourself, I have self-control — I can control the way my body moves.

Use appropriate language to encourage children to create a mental image of self-control and to reinforce this abstract concept. *I know what self-control looks like. I know what it feels like to have self-control. I know what it feels like to control my body.*

For example, the teacher says:

- You made your body move in lots of different ways. You are in charge of your own body.
- You can control the way your body moves. You have self-control.
- That took a lot of control to make yourself listen and follow my directions. You can control your body. You have self-control.
- You were so patient waiting for your turn. That took self-control to wait so quietly.
- It takes self-control to move your body with no voices.
- You are the boss of yourself!

Discuss the following questions:

- What is self-control?
- Why is self-control important?
- What does self-control look like?
- Give an example of self-control?

- How can you use self-control when others are talking?
- Name some different ways we used self-control to introduce ourselves in the circle (exercise #1).

Teaching Tip:

Remind the children that you can't control what other people say and do, but you can control the things you say and do.

Repeat this activity frequently to give children the opportunity to practice controlling their bodies. Make up your own directions for the children to follow.

This activity can be as easy or as hard as you need it to be depending on the directions you give.

Create fun and different ways for the children to move their bodies.

Activity #2: I Have Self-Control!

Students are given the opportunity to practice controlling their bodies. Students learn that they are responsible for the things they say and do.

Give your students the skills and strategies they need to control their impulses!

Materials Needed:

- Copy and print the illustrations of the following poses for the children to learn and demonstrate.
- Place them in a visible place in your classroom to remind your students to use self-control.

Quiet & Still – Standing	**Quiet & Still – Sitting**	**Put Your Body Back Together**
		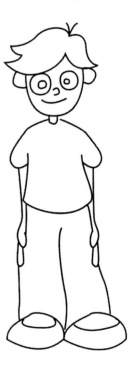

<u>Exercise #1:</u>

<u>Directions:</u>

The teacher sits on the floor in a circle with the students. Everyone sits in the circle with their legs criss-crossed.

The teacher tells the students to sit in a person-space pattern. A person-space pattern is sitting or standing with a space between your bodies so your bodies are not touching each other.

Person-Space Pattern

The teacher says, "We are going to talk about self-control. Self-control is:"

- Being able to stop your body and think before you act (or do something).
- Being in charge of your own body.
- Being able to control your body — stop and think!

"We are going to play a game. I want to see if you're strong enough to control your body. Let's see if you are in charge of your own body and if you can make your body move in different ways."

The teacher says:

(1) Let's see if you can control your voice. Everybody quietly say the word "whisper". (Students respond by quietly saying "whisper"). Using this format the teacher whispers the following words for the students to repeat:

- Softly
- Quietly
- Gently
- Smoothly
- Easy
- Calm Down
- My Body (point to yourself)
- Myself (point to yourself)
- Stop & Think
- Self-Control

The teacher says, "You can control your voice. You can make your voice talk quietly or you can make your voice louder. You're in charge of your own voice. You have self-control! Point to yourself and quietly say: I can control my voice. I have self-control. What's that called when you are in charge of your own voice — when you can control your voice?" (Self-Control). (Everyone says self-control pointing to themselves).

(2) Let's see if you can control your hands with NO VOICES.

- Everybody put your hands above your head.
- Put your hands behind your back.
- Put your hands in front of your body.
- Shake your hands as fast as you can (no voices).
- Make your hands stop.
- Make your hands wiggle from side to side.
- Make your hands stop.
- Make your hands clap loudly.
- Make your hands clap softly.
- Make your hands stop.
- Make your hands move as slow and gentle as you can.
- Make your hands stop moving.

"You can control your hands. You are in charge of your own hands. Point to yourself and quietly say: I can control my hands. I have self-control. What's that called when you are in charge of your hands — when you can control what your hands are doing?" (Self-Control). (Everyone says self-control pointing to themselves).

(3) Let's see if you can control your feet with NO VOICES.

- Everybody move your feet loud and noisy (Students stamp their feet on the floor loud and noisy).
- Make your feet stop moving.
- Control your feet and make them move softly and quietly without a sound (students tiptoe their feet quietly on the floor).
- Make your feet stop.
- Control your feet and stamp them on the floor as fast as you can.
- Make your feet stop moving.
- Control your feet and make them move as slowly as you can.
- Make your feet stop.

"You can control your feet. You can make your feet move loudly and you can make your feet move quietly. You can make your feet move fast and slow. You are in charge of your own feet. You can tell your feet what to do. Point to yourself and quietly say: I can control my feet. I have self-control. What's that called when you are in charge of your own feet and you can control them?" (Self-Control). (Everyone says self-control pointing to themselves).

(4) Let's see if you can control your head. With NO VOICES make your head:

- Look up.
- Look down.
- Move your head from side to side.
- Make your head stop moving.
- Circle your head around and around.
- Make your head stop moving.

"What's that called when you can control your head?" (Self-Control).

(5) Let's see if you can control your shoulders with NO VOICES.

- Push your shoulders up.
- Pull your shoulders down.
- Move your shoulders up and down.
- Make your shoulders stop moving.
- Circle your shoulders around and around.
- Make your shoulders stop moving.

"What's that called when you can control your shoulders?" (Self-Control).

(6) Let's see if you can control your whole body with NO VOICES? Everyone stand up in your own space. Let's stand in a person space-pattern (a space between your bodies so your bodies are not touching).

Person-Space Pattern

- With no voices — control your whole body by making it jump up and down.
- Make your body stop moving.
- With no voices — make your body tiptoe.
- Make your whole body stop moving.
- With no voices — make your body stamp your feet and clap your hands.
- Make your body stop moving.
- With no voices shake your whole body: your head, your shoulders, your arms, your hands, your legs, and your feet.
- Make your whole body stop moving.
- Shake your whole body while using loud voices (students scream and yell while moving their bodies all around).
- Stop your bodies. Stop your voices. Show me how quickly you can take control of your body and calm your body down. Stand with your bodies perfectly still.

"What's that called when you can control your whole body? (Self-Control). You can make your whole body move. You can make your body stop. You can make your body move noisily or you can make your body move quietly. You are in charge of your own body when your body listens to what you tell it to do. Point to yourself and repeat after me" (students repeat the following sentences after the teacher):

- I can control my body.
- I can control myself.
- I have self-control.
- I can control the things I say and do.

"We are going to learn a pose. A pose is when you are strong enough to hold your body in one position. We are going to learn the **Quiet & Still** pose." (Show a picture of each pose you are demonstrating).

Quiet & Still – Standing

"While standing in your **Quiet & Still** pose (the teacher practices the poses with the students) take a deep breath and calm your body."

- Breathe in the air through your nose (inhale) all the way down to your tummy and softly let the air go back out through your mouth (exhale).
- Control your breath. No one should hear your quiet breath except for yourself.

"Let's practice breathing while standing in our **Quiet & Still** poses:"

- Breathe deeply and calm your thoughts.
- Breathe deeply and calm your whole body.

Have your students take one or two deep breaths.

"Let's sit in our **Quiet & Still** poses and practice calming our bodies by breathing. Control your body by gently and quietly placing your body on the floor in your **Quiet & Still** pose."

Quiet & Still - Sitting

- Breathe deeply and calm your thoughts.
- Breathe deeply and calm your bodies.

Have your students take one or two deep breaths.

Say to yourself: *I can control my body. I know how to calm my body down. I have self-control.*

Use positive language to encourage positive behavior.

Examples:

- Everybody did a great job standing in their **Quiet & Still** poses.
- Everyone worked really hard practicing their breathing to calm their bodies.
- It is easier to make good choices when your body is feeling calm.

The teacher calls the name of one person (someone who is a positive role model) to demonstrate the **Quiet & Still** pose.

That student stands in front of the class and demonstrates the **Quiet & Still** pose. The teacher points to that student and says:

- Is John (call the name of your student) talking? No
- Is John moving? No

The teacher says, "I see self-control. I see someone who is so strong they can control their thoughts and their body. This is what self-control looks like. Let's see what it feels like to have self-control. Everyone stand in their **Quiet & Still** poses and breathe. (Have your students take one or two deep breaths). Concentrate on breathing and keeping your body still." (Students should stay in their poses for several seconds).

Quiet & Still – Standing

Put Your Body Back Together – hands by your sides and feet together. Breathe (take one or two deep breaths).

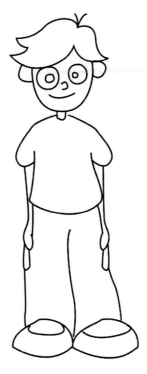

Put Your Body Back Together

"Show me your **Quiet & Still** pose – sitting. Control your body by gently and quietly placing your body on the floor in your **Quiet & Still** pose. Breathe." (Take one or two deep breaths).

While your students are sitting in their **Quiet & Still** poses, the teacher says, "I'm going to call out some different things for you to think about to yourself. Do not say them out loud. Continue breathing and sitting in your **Quiet & Still** poses while you:

- Think of your favorite color.
  (Pause for several seconds).
- Think of something you love to do.
  (Pause for several seconds).
- Think of your favorite snack.
  (Pause for several seconds).
- Think of some positive things (good choices) you could say or do if someone is teasing you.
  (Pause for several seconds).
- Think of some positive things you could say or do if someone is teasing your friend.
  (Pause for several seconds).
- What does it mean to take responsibility for the things you choose to say and do?
  (Pause for several seconds)

Give your students the opportunity to discuss their thoughts. Students should be patient by taking turns and listening while others are talking (self-control).

Next, the teacher says, "**Put Your Body Back Together**. Control your body by gently and quietly rising to a standing position to **Put Your Body Back Together.** Breathe." (Take one or two deep breaths). Students should stay in this position for several seconds.

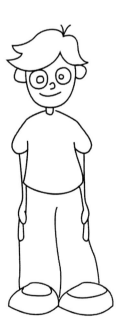

Repeat this exercise daily. The teacher should call out positive things for the children to think about while sitting in their **Quiet & Still** poses. Adapt the statements to fit the needs of your students.

After learning the poses you may want to add peaceful background music (optional) for the children to listen to while practicing the poses and breathing.

Teaching Tips:

- Students should hold their poses for at least ten seconds or whatever seems appropriate depending on their ages.
- Encourage them to concentrate on their breathing to calm their thoughts and their bodies.
- Give students the opportunity to practice these poses every day.
- Gradually lengthen the amount of time they stay in their poses to encourage self-control, concentration, and stillness — taking control of their thoughts and actions.
- Students experience what it feels like to take control of themselves by giving them the opportunity to practice calming their thoughts and their bodies. This encourages body awareness.

Exercise #2:

Directions:

The teacher says, "Let's see if you can move around the room with self-control. Move quietly with no voices."

Students all move in the same direction. The teacher calls out different ways for the students to control their bodies while moving around the room with NO VOICES:

The teacher says:

(1)   Jog (slow running) with no voices. Give students the opportunity to jog for about 30 seconds (or whatever seems appropriate depending on the age group).
(2)   Make your body stop in your **Quiet & Still – Standing** pose. Breathe and calm your body. Give students the opportunity to stay in this pose, breathe, and calm their bodies for several seconds. Vary the amount of time the students stay in their poses.
(3)   Jog with loud feet.
(4)   How quickly can you take control of your body? Show me how you can calm your bodies down by standing in your **Quiet & Still** poses and breathe (students should maintain this pose for at least ten seconds).
(5)   Control your body and jog with soft and quiet feet.
(6)   Stop and **Put Your Body Back Together.** Breathe.

Repeat numbers 1 through 6 galloping and then skipping.

"Let's see if we can control our bodies by making our bodies change from jogging to galloping to skipping without stopping."

(1)   The teacher calls out: jogging, galloping, skipping; alternating the movements. Vary the amount of time students spend jogging, galloping, or skipping before calling out a different movement.
(2)   The teacher says: stop in your **Quiet & Still – Standing** pose. Breathe. Show me how quickly you can balance in your **Quiet & Still** pose and calm your body.
(3)   **Put Your Body Back Together**. Breathe.

The teacher says, "Look at all the different ways you can make your body move. You can control your body. You are in charge of your own body. You have SELF-CONTROL!"

It's fun to do this activity with music. Choose a piece of music that's easy to jog, gallop, or skip to (optional).

<u>Teaching Tips:</u>

Consistently use positive reinforcement to encourage positive behavior in various situations.

Examples:

- You are in charge of your own body. You were walking so quietly in the hallway. You have self-control!
- You can make your body stop. You can make your body go. You can make your feet move loudly and noisily or you can make your feet move softly and quietly. You are the boss of your own body. You have self-control.
- You can control the way your body moves. You have self-control.
- That took a lot of control to make yourself listen and follow my directions. You can control your body. You have self-control.
- You were so patient waiting for your turn. That took self-control to wait so quietly.
- It takes self-control to move your body with no voices.
- I know you were feeling angry. That took self-control to calm your body down so quickly. That took self-control to use your words and say stop, I don't like that.
- You are the boss of yourself.
- You are responsible for the things you say and do.

This encourages the students to form a mental image of self-control and a connection to this abstract concept. *I know what self-control looks like. I know what it feels like to take control of my body. I know how to use self-control to control myself in a positive way.*
Consistently use the word self-control on a daily basis to reinforce this concept. For example:

- Everybody come sit in the circle with self-control. Remember, you are in charge of your own body. You are strong enough to keep your hands in your lap with no voices.
- **Put Your Body Back Together** before I give the directions.
- Let's sit in your **Quiet & Still** pose. This is what self-control looks like (sitting in the **Quiet & Still** pose).
- Let's sit in your **Quiet & Still** pose. This is what self-control feels like — being able to control your own body by sitting quietly, breathing, and calming your thoughts, and controlling your actions.
- Self-control means to stop your body and think before you act (do something)!

Exercise #3:

Directions:

Discuss the following statements and questions. They are designed to stimulate an active discussion on self-control. The answers I have provided are suggestions and will vary from student to student. After discussing the following questions have your students write their answers (1st grade and up).

(1) What is self-control?
- Being able to stop your body.
- Being able to control your body.
- Telling your body what to do.
- Being able to control your thoughts.
- Stop and think!

(2) Why is self-control important?
- It helps to make positive choices.
- It helps to calm my thoughts and my body.
- It helps to stop and think before you make a choice.

(3) What does self-control look like?
- Students may demonstrate the **Quiet & Still** pose or **Put Your Body Back Together.**
- Students may sit with their hands in their lap and look at the person who is talking.
- When you are studying and you are paying attention to what you are doing.
- If someone is teasing me I use my self-control to look confident and stay calm. I look them in the eye and say stop, I don't like that.

(4) Give an example of self-control.
- Waiting for my turn.
- Being patient.
- Sitting in my **Quiet & Still** pose to calm my body when I'm feeling angry.
- Knowing that I have to study instead of going out with my friends.

(5) How can you use self-control when others are talking?
- By controlling my voice and waiting for the other person to finish talking.
- By controlling my ears and listening to what the other person is saying before I begin talking.
- By telling myself I will not interrupt the person talking. I can control my voice.

(6) Show me the **Quiet & Still** pose.
- Students demonstrate the **Quiet & Still** pose sitting and standing.

(7) How can practicing the **Quiet & Still** pose help you to take control of the things you say and do?
- It helps me to calm my body when I sit quietly before I make a choice.
- It gives me time to stop and think before I do something.
- Breathing while I am in my **Quiet & Still** pose gives me time to calm my body down and think.
- It's easier to make a positive choice when I am calm.
- It reminds me to think about the feelings of others.

(8) Show me **Put Your Body Back Together**.
- Students demonstrate this pose.

(9) What does the pose **Put Your Body Back Together mean?**
- It reminds me to keep my hands to myself.
- It reminds me to take control of my thoughts and actions.

(10) How can practicing the **Quiet & Still** pose help to calm your body?
- When I'm upset and I sit in my **Quiet & Still** pose and breathe it helps my body relax and not feel so tight.
- When I'm feeling mad my body feels good when I stop and calm down.
- It helps me to stay out of trouble when I take time to stop and think before I do something.
- The more I practice, the better I get at calming my thoughts and my body and — the more confident I feel in myself.

(11) Sit in your **Quiet & Still** pose (about 30 seconds or whatever seems appropriate depending on the age of your students). What were you thinking about or saying to yourself, while sitting in your **Quiet & Still** pose, to help keep your body quiet and still?
- When I think about playing with my dog it makes me feel happy and calm.
- When I think about dancing it makes me feel happy.
- When I concentrate on my breathing and pay attention to my body I begin to feel calm.

(12) Why is it important to calm your thoughts and your body before you decide what to do?
- It helps to make a good choice when you are calm.
- It's easier to make a good choice when you stop and think before you do something.

Teaching Tips:

- Give students the opportunity to practice controlling their bodies, moving their bodies from a hyper state to being quiet and still. *I know what self-control looks like. I know what self-control feels like.*
- Practice these poses daily to increase mental/emotional strength and body awareness. This encourages the connection between the body and mind. *I know how to calm my thoughts and my body.*
- Encourage students to take control of their bodies by focusing on their thoughts and their actions.
- Give students the opportunity to calm their bodies by practicing their breathing, while sitting or standing, in their **Quiet & Still** poses.
- The more opportunities they are given to practice controlling their bodies and expressing themselves in a positive way, the more competent they become with self-control.
- Practice inspires confidence when students feel they are capable of controlling their bodies (actions).
- Remind your students — you can control the things you say and do!

Repeat these activities. Use your own creativity by coming up with different ways for your students to move their bodies and then calm their bodies by sitting or standing in their **Quiet & Still** poses.

The key to self-control is practice, practice, practice!

Activity #3: What is Focus?

Directions:

The teacher explains that focus means to look at something or someone and to think about what you are doing and looking at.

Exercise #1:

The teacher calls out the following directions for the children to demonstrate. Remind the children to use their self-control while focusing — move your body with no voices.

The teacher says everyone focus:

- On your hands.
- On your foot.
- On your knee.
- On your elbow.
- On the person talking.
- On your fingers.
- On a color (name a color in the room). How do you know it's red? (Because I'm focusing on it).
- On an object (name an object in the room) and describe it.
- In front of you.
- To the side of your body.
- On me. What color is my shirt, shoes, etc?
- On your right hand.
- On your left foot.
- On your wrist.
- Between your hands.
- Between your foot and the floor.
- Up.
- Down.
- Behind you.
- Your arm.

The teacher demonstrates different movements and tells the children to focus on what he or she is doing.

The teacher says, "Focus on my body."

The teacher asks:
- What is my body (jumping) doing? How do you know my body is jumping? (Because I'm focusing on you).
- What is my body (bending) doing? How do you know my body is bending? (Because I'm watching you. I'm focusing on you).

The teacher says, "Focus on my hands."

The teacher asks:
- What are my hands (clapping) doing? How do you know my hands are clapping? (Because I'm focusing on you).
- What are my hands (shaking) doing? How do you know my hands are shaking? (Because I'm focusing on you).

The teacher says, "Focus on my feet."

The teacher asks:
- What are my feet (tiptoeing) doing? How do you know my feet are tiptoeing?
- What are my feet (stomping) doing? How do you know my feet are stomping?

Exercise #2:

The teacher calls out different things around the room for the children to focus on and describe.

For example, focus on a:

- Chair
- Chalkboard
- Clock
- Book

The teacher discusses "focus" with the students by asking the following questions:

- What does it mean to focus?
- Why is it important to focus on what you are doing?
- What happens when you are not focusing on what you are doing?
- How does self-control help you to focus?

Teaching Tips:

After introducing the word focus and it's meaning begin using it every day in conversational speech. For example:

- Please focus on me because I need to give you the directions.
- Please focus on Mr. Johnson because he is going to tell us about career day.
- Please pay attention and focus on me while I'm telling the story.

When children hear the words "pay attention" and "focus" used in the same context they know what they are supposed to do when they hear these words. *When I hear the words "pay attention" and "focus" I'm supposed to look at the person who is talking and think about what I'm supposed to be doing.*

This gives children the opportunity to practice focusing and reinforces this abstract concept. *I know what it looks like to focus (pay attention). I know what it feels like to focus (pay attention).*

Activity #4: Learning to Focus

Materials Needed:

- Various objects of different sizes, shapes, colors, and textures.
- Flashlight.

Directions:

Place various objects around the room such as a book, ball, box, vase, key, etc. Use objects that are different sizes, colors, shapes, textures, and weights. Turn out the lights. Shine a flashlight on each object you want the children to focus on.

The teacher asks various questions, such as:

- What are you focusing on?
- What color is it?
- What shape is it?
- What do you use it for?
- Does it look like it would be heavy or light?
- Does it look soft, rough, or smooth?
- Describe what you are focusing on.

Teaching Tip:

Remind the children to stop and think! Instead of yelling out the name of the object, children have to control their impulses by waiting for their name to be called before they can answer the questions.

After focusing on the objects give children the opportunity to touch the objects and discuss the way they look and feel.

The teacher asks the following questions. Suggested answers are in parenthesis.

- How did you learn all of this information about those objects? (By focusing).
- What does it mean to focus on what you are doing? (To look at what you are doing and think about what you are doing).
- How does self-control help you to focus? (Self-control is being in charge of your body. I can make my eyes focus on the person who is talking).
- How do you use self-control to stop and think before you act? (By controlling my body. Making my body stop, calm down, and think before I do something).
- How did you use self-control to wait for your name to be called before you could answer the question? (By controlling my body to be patient and wait for my turn).

Activity #5: Mental/Emotional & Physical Strength

This activity gives your students the opportunity to experience the difference between mental strength and physical strength. It gives them an understanding of the importance of mental strength and how it can be used to overcome obstacles and accomplish your goals.

Materials Needed:

- A picture of the inside of the body that shows the brain and the muscles.
- A piece of elastic about twelve inches long.

Directions:

The teacher asks:

"What is the difference between mental/emotional strength and physical strength? Physical strength is having a strong body. If you could look inside your body what would you see? Muscles (show & discuss the picture that shows the muscles inside the body)."

Next, show the piece of elastic. "This is what our muscles look like. Let's see what our muscles look like when we stretch them (demonstrate by stretching the elastic). When we stretch our muscles we make our bodies long. When we stop stretching our muscles relax (gently release the elastic). Let's stretch our hands, fingers, arms, legs, and back. Let's stretch our whole bodies. (Give your students a few minutes to stretch their bodies)."

Tell your students to stretch their muscles like the elastic. Stretching helps to relax our bodies. When we stretch our muscles it makes our bodies strong. When we exercise our bodies we strengthen these muscles and build physical strength.

Name and discuss different ways to build physical strength. Examples:

- Swimming
- Lifting Weights
- Jogging

Give students the opportunity to jog, exercise, or stretch to demonstrate physical strength.

For example, tell your students to:

- Jog in place for one minute.
- Skip in place for one minute.
- Do ten jumping jacks.

When we exercise our bodies we build physical strength.

The teacher explains that mental and emotional strength are having a strong brain, mind, and positive thoughts (show and discuss the picture of the brain inside the body). Your brain controls your body. Your brain tells your body what to do.

What are positive thoughts? Positive thoughts are all the good things we think about and say to ourselves (self-talk). Self-talk is when you say positive things to yourself. Let's think of some positive thoughts.

Examples:

- I am the boss of my own body.
- Sharing, thoughtfulness, kindness.
- Stop and think.
- Breathe and calm down.
- I will not let those words get to me.
- I can control my body.
- I have self-control. I can control my actions.
- I am strong enough to tell someone how I feel.
- I am strong enough to ask for help.
- I am smart!
- I am a great person!
- I believe in myself!

We keep our positive thoughts inside our brain. Self-control is using these positive thoughts to control our body. Positive thoughts build mental and emotional strength.

We need to exercise our brains to build mental/emotional strength just like we need to exercise our bodies to build physical strength.

Give students the opportunity to demonstrate mental/emotional strength by participating in the following exercises. Tell the children to sit on the floor in a circle in a person-space pattern (a space between their bodies so their bodies are not touching).

Exercise #1:

The teacher gives the following directions:

- Sit with your legs extended straight out in front of your body.
- Cross your legs.
- Pull your legs towards your body into a crisscrossed position.
- Cross your arms over your chest.
- Keep your bottom glued to the floor and roll your tummy up. Your back should be straight and your shoulders down (good posture). This is what good body form and posture looks like and feels like.
- Look what happens when you drop your tummy. Your back and shoulders fall down too. This creates a messy, slouched body (bad posture).
- Let's practice sitting in our **Quiet and Still** poses and alternate rolling our tummies up (proper body form) and rolling our tummies down (messy/sloppy bodies). (This creates body awareness by giving children the opportunity to feel the correct placement of their bodies).

Quiet & Still

- Sit correctly in your **Quiet and Still** pose. Pull your tummy up, backs straight, and shoulders down.
- Focus straight in front of yourself.
- Breathe. Take a deep breath by breathing in the air through your nose (inhale) all the way down to your tummy and softly let the air go back out through your mouth (exhale). Control your breath. No one should hear your quiet breath except for yourself.
- Breathe in (inhale) a long, slow, steady stream of air into your body. Gently blow the air out of your mouth (exhale).

Select peaceful background music (optional) for the children to listen to while relaxing in their **Quiet & Still** poses. Tell the children to control their bodies and — breathe in all of their positive thoughts and gently blow away all of the negative thoughts. *I know what self-control looks like. I know what self-control feels like.*

Use your mental/emotional strength to take control of your body. Take a deep breath and say to yourself:

• I am strong enough to calm my body by breathing.
• I am strong enough to control the things I say and do.

This is a great exercise to practice every day to increase mental/emotional strength and body awareness. This exercise encourages mind-body coordination by giving you the opportunity to communicate with yourself and connect to your feelings.

Discuss this question. Why do we sit in our **Quiet & Still** poses?

• To calm our thoughts and our bodies.
• To hear ourselves think.
• To stop and think.
• To keep our bodies and minds healthy.
• To breathe, relax, and stay calm.
• To think clearly.
• To strengthen our brains or to build mental strength.
• To think about the way our body feels.
• To think about the way others feel.

The teacher asks:

• Why is it important to calm our thoughts and our bodies before we make a choice?

Exercise #2:

Materials Needed:

- Copy and print the illustrations of the following poses.

Directions:

Teach your students the following poses to practice self-control and focus. Remember, self-control and focus build mental and emotional strength. Use your positive thoughts to stay focused and control your body.

Remind your students to use good posture when balancing in the poses.

- Always stand or sit tall.
- Pull your tummy up.
- Your back should be straight and your shoulders down.
- Focus straight in front of yourself.
- Take deep breaths.
- Concentrate on yourself, what you are doing, and how your body feels.
- Balance in each pose for about ten seconds.

Let's begin with the **Quiet & Still** pose. Take a deep breath.

Quiet & Still - sitting

Gently move your hands into the **Peace** pose. Take a deep breath.

Peace

Control your body by gently and quietly rising to a standing position and balance in the **Sideways** pose. Take a deep breath.

Sideways

Control your body by gently and quietly placing your body on the floor and balance in the **Lift** pose. Take a deep breath.

Lift

Control your body by gently and quietly moving your body into the **L** pose and balance. Take a deep breath.

L

Control your body by gently and quietly returning to the **Quiet & Still** pose. Take a deep breath.

Quiet & Still - sitting

<u>Exercise #3:</u>

<u>Materials Needed:</u>

- Bubbles, soft sponges, or feathers.

<u>Directions:</u>

To increase the level of difficulty, the teacher creates distractions. The teacher blows bubbles all around their bodies while the students are balancing in the poses from exercise #2. Students use their mental strength to continue balancing while being distracted by the bubbles.

The teacher can also toss soft sponges or feathers towards the students to try and distract them while balancing. Encourage students to use their mental strength to stay focused on what they are doing and maintain their balance while others are trying to distract them.

The goal is to experience self-control, focus, and concentration. This enhances the connection between the body and mind through mental, emotional, and body awareness.

Encourage students to use positive self-talk to stay focused on what they are doing while they are balancing, for example, saying these words to yourself: *I will not let the bubbles distract me or I will stay focused on what I'm doing. I can control my body.*

Discuss the following question with your students:

What did you do to ignore the bubbles (the distraction)? Or what did you say to yourself to stay focused on balancing and concentrating on what you were doing?

<u>Exercise #4:</u>

<u>Directions:</u>

The teacher explains that self-talk is saying positive thoughts to yourself. When teaching self-talk, tell your students to:

- Say their positive words out loud three times, for example, *I am confident.*
- Next, whisper these same words three times to yourself, *I am confident.*
- Say these same words to yourself with your mouth closed (no voices).
- Repeat *I am confident* to yourself three times without a sound.

Examples of positive self-talk to discuss and practice with your students:

- I will use my words to say how I feel.
- I will not use violence.
- I am strong enough to tell an adult.
- I will use my mental strength to say to myself, I am confident, calm, and focused.
- I can do this.
- I believe in myself!

Discuss the following questions then have your students write the answers (1st grade and up). They are designed to stimulate an active discussion on how to handle various situations. The answers I have provided are suggestions and will vary from student to student.

(1) What should you do if someone was teasing you and hurt your feelings with their words? I would say to myself:

- I will not let those words get to me, walk away, and play with another friend.
- Respond with confidence, good posture, maintain eye contact, and say: stop, I don't like that.

(2) What should you NOT do if someone is teasing you? Why?

- Cry.
- Lose my self-control by fighting back with unkind words and showing I am out of control.

(3) What should you do if you feel that someone was going to hurt you or someone else?

- Tell an adult.

(4) How does mental/emotional strength give you the power to handle difficult situations, such as being teased?

- It gives me the strength to stay calm and control my actions.

(5) How do you feel when you can control your thoughts and actions?

- Strong
- Confident

(6) Why do we sit in the **Quiet & Still** pose or the **Peace** pose?

- To calm our thoughts and our bodies.
- To stop and think.
- To breathe, relax, and stay calm.
- To build mental/emotional strength.
- To think about the way our bodies feel.
- To think about the way others feel.
- To practice positive self-talk and focus.

(7)   How can exercising every day build physical strength?

   • The more you exercise, the stronger your muscles get.

(8)   How can using positive thoughts (self-talk) every day help you to build mental/emotional strength?

   • The more I practice using positive thoughts, the better I get at controlling my actions.

(9)   Name some ways to build emotional/mental strength.

   Practice:
   • Self-Control
   • Focus
   • Self-Talk
   • Balancing
   • Sitting in the **Quiet & Still** or **Peace** pose

(10)   Why is it important to practice self-control, focus, and using positive thoughts?

   • The more I practice, the better I get at controlling myself.
   • The more I practice, the better I get at stopping and thinking.

Classroom Suggestions:

   • Have your students practice self-talk daily to build self-esteem, confidence, a positive self-image, and mental/emotional strength while sitting in the **Peace** pose.
   • Keep a positive thoughts jar in your classroom. Students write positive thoughts on a strip of paper and place them in the jar. Someone picks a positive thought from the jar and reads it to the class every day. Students repeat the positive thought out loud and then to themselves.
   • For younger children, the teacher can help them write their positive thoughts. The teacher and the children can read their positive thoughts together.

<u>Activity #6:</u> <u>Organizing Your Thoughts:</u>

<u>Materials Needed:</u>

- A set of five index cards for each child. Each set of cards is numbered one (1) through five (5). Each card has one number written on it.

<u>Directions:</u>

The teacher asks, "What does it mean to organize your thoughts or put your thoughts in order?"

Organizing your thoughts means to:

- Stop and think.
- Make a plan.
- Put your thoughts and ideas in order. Ask yourself, *what do I need to do first?*
- Carry out your thoughts and ideas to accomplish your goals.

<u>Exercise #1:</u>

The teacher says, "Let's count to five in order. One, two, three, four, five. When you count to five in order, the numbers are organized and in the correct order from one to five."

Ask the children, "Are these numbers organized and in the correct order? Two, five, one, four, three? No, they are unorganized. They are not in the correct order."

Give each child a set of five index cards numbered one through five. Mix up the cards. Tell the children their cards represent their thoughts. Have the children organize their cards (their thoughts) by putting them in the correct order, one through five.

When your thoughts are unorganized (like numbers that are unorganized) your body doesn't know what to do first. When you organize your thoughts you put your ideas in order and your body knows what to do. Organizing your thoughts helps you to think clearly. When you organize your thoughts you have to stop and think, *what should I do first?*

Exercise #2: Glitter Jar

Materials Needed:

- A saltshaker filled with glitter.
- A medium-sized clear plastic jar.
- A to Z, Do You Ever Feel Like Me? By Bonnie Hausman or any other book on feelings. You may also use pictures of children displaying a variety of emotions.

Directions:

Read the book A to Z, Do You Ever Feel Like Me by Bonnie Hausman or show and discuss pictures of children displaying many different feelings.

After showing the pictures and discussing one's feelings, the teacher tells the children, "We experience many different thoughts and feelings throughout the day. Let's name some thoughts and feelings, for example, sometimes I feel happy, sad, excited, scared, or frustrated."

The teacher shows the saltshaker filled with glitter. Tell the children the glitter represents their thoughts and feelings. The teacher passes the shaker to each child giving them the opportunity to sprinkle their thoughts and feelings into the medium-sized clear jar. Tell the children the jar represents their bodies. After everyone has sprinkled their feelings (glitter) into the jar (their bodies), the teacher adds more glitter to represent lots of different feelings (make sure the bottom of the jar is covered with the glitter).

The teacher adds water to the jar then briskly shakes it. When the teacher stops shaking the jar the children watch their thoughts (represented by the glitter) as they swirl around: confused, fast, and furious inside their bodies (the jar).

This gives children the opportunity to see what their thoughts and feelings look like when they are unorganized or out of control. The children continue to watch their thoughts and feelings as they begin to calm, slow down, and eventually stop as they settle inside the jar (their bodies).

The teacher tells the children to sit in their **Quiet & Still** poses, stop their bodies, and take a deep breath. Your mind becomes clear just like the water when your thoughts are calm. You can now see clearly so you can think and organize your thoughts. Stop, think, breathe, and organize your thoughts so your body knows what to do.

Give children their own clear plastic jars to sprinkle their thoughts (glitter) inside. When children need to calm down or your classroom becomes to loud give children the opportunity to take a body break. Tell your students to:

- Shake their thoughts and feelings jar and place it in front of them.
- Sit in the **Quiet & Still** or **Peace** pose and breathe.

Tell the children to focus on their thoughts and feelings jar as they calm their bodies while watching and feeling their thoughts as they settle inside their bodies.

The teacher discusses with the children why it's important to calm your thoughts and your bodies before you make a choice.

The teacher asks the following questions. You may need to adapt the questions to fit the needs of your students. Remind them to stop, think, and organize their thoughts before they answer.

- How do you wash your hands? Why do you wash your hands?
- How do you brush your teeth? Why do you brush your teeth?
- How do you make your bed? Why do you make your bed?
- How do you make a sandwich?
- What should you do if someone called you a name that you didn't like?
- What should you do if a stranger said: *I have some puppies I want to show you in my car?*
- What should you do if a stranger said: *Would you like some candy?*
- What should you do if a stranger said: *Would you help me look for my dog?*
- How can organizing your thoughts help you to make a positive choice?
- Why do we organize our thoughts?
- Why is it important to stop and think?

Exercise #3:

Materials Needed:

- Suggested Reading: A to Z, Do You Ever Feel Like Me? By Bonnie Hausman. If this book is not available, you can use pictures of children displaying a variety of emotions.

Directions:

Discuss the different feelings/emotions in the book, Do You Ever Feel Like Me? By Bonnie Hausman.

Have one person choose an emotion or feeling from the book. That person illustrates the feeling through the movement of their body. The other children guess what feeling they are demonstrating.

The teacher asks various questions about the emotions that the children are demonstrating to encourage a discussion about feelings.

For example, if someone is demonstrating what their body looks like when they are feeling angry, the teacher might ask:

- What kind of things make you feel angry?
- Describe how your body is feeling when you are angry.
- How can you control your actions when you are feeling angry?
- What can you do to calm your body down when you are feeling angry?
- Why should you calm your body down when you are feeling angry before you make a choice?

This encourages body awareness. It teaches children to recognize and acknowledge how their bodies are moving and feeling when they are experiencing different emotions. It also encourages children to recognize and acknowledge the feelings of others.

Activity #7: Self-Control, Cooperation, & Body Awareness

Materials Needed:

- Pieces of string (about fourteen inches long) - You will need enough strings for each person to share with a partner.
- Streamers (about fourteen inches long) - You will need enough streamers for each person to share with a partner.

Directions:

The teacher explains that self-control is being able to stop your body and think before you act. Self-control is being in charge of your own body. Remember to stop and think before you move your body. Stop and think before you decide what to do.
Cooperation is getting along with others.

Exercise #1:

Each child has a partner. Encourage the children to cooperate with each other by having them perform the following commands. Tell the children to think of different ways you and your partner can demonstrate:

- Jumping together.
- Being polite to each other.
- Shaking hands with each other.

- Moving slowly together.
- Moving with good posture.
- Moving while holding hands.

Next, the teacher explains that instead of holding hands, each partner will hold the end of the piece of string (about fourteen inches long).
The teacher calls out different ways for them to move together while holding on to the string, such as:

- Walking
- Galloping
- Jogging

- Skipping
- Moving backwards
- Jumping

The teacher asks:

- How did you cooperate with your partner to move together?
- Why didn't the string break when you were holding on to it?

Next, give them a streamer to hold on to. Partners hold each end of the streamer while moving together in different ways. Tell the children to pay attention to the way they have to control their bodies while they are moving together so they do not tear the streamer.

Ask the following questions:

- How did you need to move your body while holding on to the streamer with your partner without tearing it?
- Did you have to move your bodies differently when you were holding on to the string?

Give children other objects to hold on to with their partners while moving in different ways, such as a feather, a beanbag, or a balloon.

Discuss with the children the different ways they had to cooperate with each other and control their bodies, not to tear or drop the objects, while moving.

Exercise #2:

Materials Needed:

- A tin filled with marbles or ping-pong balls.

Directions:

For this activity you will use the tin filled with marbles or ping-pong balls. Tell the children to sit in a circle in a person-space pattern (a small space between their bodies so they are not touching each other).

Tell the children they are in control of the sound of the marbles. The children have to control the movement of their bodies to pass the tin of marbles around the circle loudly or quietly.

First, give them the opportunity to pass the tin around the circle loudly. Discuss with the children the type of movement used to create a loud sound with the tin. For example, I passed the tin fast using strong arms to make a loud noise.

Next, instruct the children to pass the tin of marbles around the circle without a sound. Discuss with the children the type of movement used to create a quiet sound or silence.

Children need to concentrate and focus on their bodies to control their movements. For example, children need to move their bodies softly, slowly, and gently when passing the tin to create a quiet sound or silence. Everyone cooperates by trying to pass the tin of marbles around the circle without a sound.

Create different ways for the children to practice controlling their bodies to move the tin of marbles quietly.

Suggestions: Without a sound move the tin of marbles:

- Above your head.
- Place it on the floor.
- Turning in a circle.
- Walking.

Ask the children:

- What is self-control?
- How did you use self-control and focus to pass the tin of marbles quietly?
- Name some different ways you can move your body to create a quiet movement.
- How can self-control help you to use polite words or good manners?
- How can self-control help you to make positive choices?
- Why is it important to use self-control?
- How can you use self-control when you are feeling angry?
- Why is it important to stop and think before you say or do something?

Teaching Tip:

This activity encourages body awareness. It encourages children to be aware of how they have to control their bodies to create various movements. It also creates awareness of the movement of others.

Activity #8: Self-Control, Focus, & Positive Thoughts

Materials Needed:

- Copy and print the illustration of the **Bow & Arrow** pose.

Directions:

The teacher tells the children to focus on the **Bow & Arrow** pose:

Bow & Arrow

Exercise #1:

The teacher asks the following questions while the children are focusing on the **Bow & Arrow** pose.

- Where are his hands?
- Are his fingers together or separated?
- Is his back straight or crooked?
- Are his arms straight or crooked?

- How many body parts is he balancing on?
- What body part is he balancing on?
- What direction is his knee facing?
- How many triangles do you see in this pose?

The teacher tells the children to concentrate and balance in the **Bow & Arrow** pose. Focus straight in front of yourself. Concentrate and balance in the **Bow & Arrow** pose on the other foot.

Encourage the children to maintain their balance for at least ten seconds. Older children should hold their balance for at least thirty seconds.

Teaching Tips:

Before balancing in the **Bow & Arrow** pose remind the children to:

- Take a deep breath.
- Stop and think. Think about the way your body feels.
- Ask yourself, *how should I move my body?*

After balancing in the **Bow & Arrow** pose the teacher asks:

- What did you think about and concentrate on to help you balance?
- How did self-control, focus, and positive thoughts help you to balance?
- How did self-control, focus, and positive thoughts help you to control your body?

For younger children the pose does not have to be perfect. The goal is to encourage and experience self-control and focus through body awareness.

Use positive language to describe the children's actions. Positive language encourages positive behavior.

Examples of Positive Language:

- You are keeping your body still while balancing. That takes self-control.
- You are working so hard trying to balance. It takes practice to learn new things.
- I can see you are getting frustrated trying to balance. It's ok to make a mistake. What can you do to relax and calm your body before you try again?
- You are really controlling your body to balance. You know how to concentrate and focus on what you are doing.
- You are looking at me while I'm giving you the directions. You know how to focus on the person who is talking.
- You are so quiet while I'm talking. You are in charge of your voice. What's that called when you can control your body? (self-control)

Repeat this activity by using other poses to focus on, describe, and demonstrate, such as, yoga or the poses and moving balances from the book *Discover ME.*

Exercise #2:

Materials Needed:

- One piece of blue construction paper.
- One piece of red construction paper.
- A peace sign (drawn on a piece of construction paper).
- Masking tape.

Directions:

The teacher places small pieces of masking tape randomly around the room. Each child stands on a piece of tape. The teacher says, "Focus on me to WATCH for the directions."

- When the teacher holds up the color blue, the children leave their tape and move around the room in various ways while focusing on this color. The teacher calls out different ways for the children to move, such as walking, galloping, jogging, skipping, etc. Children maintain their focus on the color blue while moving around the room.
- When the teacher holds up the color red, children calmly return to their tape and move in place while focusing on the color red.
- When the teacher holds up the peace sign, children calm their bodies by sitting in the **Quiet & Still** pose on their piece of tape. Children control their bodies by placing themselves on the floor without a sound.

Children continue to focus on the teacher while moving their bodies and while sitting in their **Quiet & Still** poses to WATCH for the directions. When moving around the room children should always move in the same direction. Add music for the children to move to (optional).

<u>Teaching Tip:</u>

Remind the children when you see the color:

- Blue – Move around the room. The teacher calls out various ways to move, such as jogging or galloping.
- Red – Return to your tape and continue moving your body in place.
- Peace Sign – Sit on your tape in the **Quiet & Still** pose and take deep breaths.

This encourages children to focus and maintain eye contact. Repeat this activity by presenting different pictures or objects for the children to focus on.

If using detailed pictures for the children to focus on while moving around the room, ask them to discuss and describe the pictures they focused on.

Activity #9: Peace

Materials Needed:

- Copy and print the illustrations of the following poses for the children to learn and demonstrate.

Directions:

Write the numbers 1, 2, 3, 4 on a sheet of construction paper. On another sheet of paper write the numbers 5, 6, 7, 8. Make sure to write the numbers large enough so they can be seen from a distance.

Exercise #1:

Tell the children to sit in the **Peace** pose. Remind them to roll their tummies up, keep their backs straight, and their shoulders down. (Show what it looks like and feels like to be peaceful and confident in yourself).

Peace

The teacher says, "Take a deep breath (while counting to yourself 1, 2, 3, 4) breathing in the air through your nose (inhaling) all the way down to your tummy. Softly let the air go back out (while counting 5, 6, 7, 8) through your mouth (exhaling). Control your breath. No one should hear your quiet breath except for yourself."

- When the children breathe in (inhale), the teacher holds up the paper with the numbers 1, 2, 3, and 4 written on it. Tell them to focus on the numbers as they slowly count to themselves while breathing in.
- When the children breathe out (exhale), the teacher holds up the paper with the numbers 5, 6, 7, and 8 written on it. Tell them to focus on the numbers as they slowly count to themselves while breathing all their air out.
- Breathe in (inhale) a long, slow, steady stream of air into your bodies. Gently blow the air out of your mouth (exhale).

After the children understand the rhythm of their breathing and counting, take the numbers away and let them practice breathing and counting to themselves.

The children sit in the **Peace** pose and take one or two deep breaths. Gradually extend the length of time they sit in this pose. Encourage the children to focus on their positive thoughts and the way their bodies feel (calm & relaxed).

The teacher tells the children to make a **Circle of Peace** in front of their bodies. Slowly lift your **Circle of Peace** above your head.

Circle of Peace

Open your peace circle stretching your arms out to the sides of your body to illustrate giving peace to others.

Giving Peace

The teacher gives the following directions:

- While sitting in the **Peace** pose, breathe in (inhale) and count 1, 2, 3, 4, at the same time you lift your **Circle of Peace** above your head. Arms stay in a circle.
- Arms open on 5 (as you exhale) and count 6, 7, and hands touch on 8 as your arms form a circle back in your lap.

Repeat the above exercise: **Peace**, the **Circle of Peace**, and **Giving Peace**. Take one or two deep breaths while practicing the peace sequence.

The teacher asks the following questions:

- When your peace circle is above your head what number do you count? 4.
- What number do you count when you open your arms? 5.
- What numbers do you count to demonstrate giving peace to others? 6 & 7.
- What number do you count when your arms form a circle and your hands are touching in your lap? 8.

Exercise #2:

Teach children the Peace Pledge. You may want to shorten the Peace Pledge by teaching only the first five lines, depending on the age of the children.

Peace Pledge

I believe in peace.
Peace begins within yourself.
I promise to be kind, thoughtful, and respectful to others.
I believe in peace.
Peace for you and me.
P is for power — the power of peace.
P is for possibilities. I promise to follow my dreams.
P is for perseverance. I promise to never give up.
E is for ethical. I promise to be fair, honest, and good.
A is for advocate. I promise to work hard for peace.
C is for control — self-control. I promise to take responsibility for the things I say and do.
E is for equal. We are all created equal.
I believe in peace.
Peace for you and me.

Discuss peace with the children.

- What is peace?
- Where does peace begin?
- Why does peace begin within yourself?
- Name some different ways you can show peace, such as:
  - A hug.
  - A handshake.
  - Talking with nice words.
  - Using self-control.
  - Sharing.
- How can you create peace on the playground?
- How can you create peace wherever you go?

Activity #10: Stop & Think!

Directions:

The teacher explains that self-control is being able to stop and think! The teacher describes an object in the room. When the children have figured out what the object is from the teacher's description, they have to write the name of the object down.

If the children cannot write the name of the object, tell them to raise their hands and wait for their name to be called.

Instead of yelling out the name of the object children have to take control of their impulses by either waiting for their name to be called or writing the answer down. This encourages children to stop and think before they act.

Teaching Tip:

Remember to use positive reinforcement to encourage positive behavior by describing their actions with the appropriate language, for example:

- That takes self-control to stop and think.
- You are really focusing on being patient. That takes self-control to wait for your turn.

The teacher asks the following questions:

- Why is it important to stop and think before you decide what to do?
- Why is it important to calm your body down before you decide what to do?
- Name some ways you can calm your body down before you act.

This activity gives children the opportunity to practice these essential skills — stop & think before you act!

Activity #11: Listening

Directions:

The teacher says to the children, "The secret of listening is to hear and remember. Even though you can't see the words, you focus (pay attention) on the words you hear. Listen to my words and remember what you are supposed to do. Use your self-control to make your body stay perfectly still until I have finished giving the directions. Stop and think before you act."

The teacher explains that, "pay attention" means to stop, look, and listen. Stop your body, look at the person who is talking, and listen to the words.

If necessary, repeat the directions one at a time. This activity can be as simple or as hard as you need it to be depending on the age of the children and the directions you give.

The teacher says:

- Touch your head, clap two times, then put your hands behind your back.
  - ➢ What was the last thing you did?
  - ➢ What was the first thing you did?
  - ➢ What was the second thing you did?
- Put one hand far away from your head and cross your feet. Stay in this position and put your other hand near your feet.
- Jump quietly two times, bounce your shoulders once; sit in the **Quiet & Still** pose.
- At the same time put one hand to the side of your body and your other hand up. Stay in this position and focus on your feet.
- Balance on three body parts.
- Jump quietly four times then jump loudly twice.
- Lift one foot near the floor and focus on your foot. Put both hands behind your back and balance.
- Tap your foot with the opposite hand then stretch both arms above your head. Circle the body part at the end of your arms.

- Focus up, focus down, and turn your body around.
- Slowly stretch one arm to the side of your body. Quickly stretch your other arm high above your head. Stay in this position and slowly lift one foot off the floor. Focus and concentrate on balancing.
- At the same time, forcefully step forward on one foot and push both hands out in front of your body.
- Quietly and gently step backward on your right foot. Stamp your left foot loudly one time. Slowly stretch both arms out to the sides of your body. Lift your heels and balance. Focus and concentrate on keeping your body still.
- With no voices control your hands and shake them as fast as you can. Make your hands stop. Control your hands and your arms by gently and slowly floating them all around your body.
- Stand in your **Quiet & Still** pose. Take a deep breath.

The teacher asks the following questions:

- What does it mean and why is it important to *"focus on the words you hear?"*
- What does it mean to *"pay attention to others?"*
- What does it mean to *"pay attention to yourself?"*
- Why is it important to listen while others are talking?

Activity #12: Self-Talk

Materials Needed:

For this activity you will need large paper cups. Each cup should be filled with the same objects, such as a:

- Button
- Paper Clip
- Penny
- Crayon
- Plastic Spoon
- Straw
- Marble

You will also need a towel to cover the objects. Each child and the teacher should have their own cup with the same objects in each one.

For example, if you have ten children and one teacher you will need eleven cups filled with the same objects.

The teacher should make a list of the different objects being used (for the teacher's use only).

Directions:

This activity teaches children to communicate with themselves (self-talk). Tell the children to sit in a circle in a person-space pattern (a small space between each person).

The teacher says, "Self-talk is when I tell myself what to do. When I repeat the directions to myself, it helps me to remember what I'm supposed to do. Self-talk is when I say positive things to myself." Encourage children to say to themselves what they are supposed to do.

Next, the teacher explains that a sequence is placing things in a certain order. The teacher chooses various objects from his or her cup to place in a sequence for the children to see (focus on). For example, the teacher places a button, marble, penny, and a crayon on the floor. Tell the children to focus on these objects and remember the correct sequence or order.

Give children a few seconds to focus on the objects. When time is up the teacher covers the objects with a cloth or towel so the children cannot see them. When the teacher says "begin" the children are instructed to take a deep breath and stop & think before they act.

Next, the children take the objects from their cups and form the same sequence from memory.

Teaching Tip:

Remind the children, focus means to look at something and to think about what you are doing and looking at. Encourage the children to concentrate on the objects they are focusing on and repeat the sequence to themselves (self-talk) to help them remember the correct order.

Always tell the children it's ok to make a mistake. It takes practice to learn new things. When finished tell the children to sit in their **Peace** poses and think of positive thoughts to say to themselves (self-talk).

Examples of Self-Talk:

- I worked hard.
- I did a good job.
- I know how to focus.

- I didn't do this correctly, but it's ok to make a mistake.
- I'm going to work harder next time.
- The more I practice, the better I get.

Encourage the children to think of other positive thoughts to say to themselves. Positive self-talk encourages confidence — believing in yourself!

Variation #1:

Directions:

The teacher refers to the list of objects being used. The teacher calls out various objects from the list in a sequence for the children to hear and remember.

Remind the children, "You can't see my words so what are you going to focus on? You are going to pay attention and concentrate on the words you hear. Listen and remember the correct order (sequence) of the objects."

Example:

The teacher calls out: button, penny, marble, napkin. When the teacher has finished saying the sequence, the children take out those objects from their cups and place them in the correct order.

Remind the children to control their impulses. Children wait until the teacher has finished calling out the sequence before they begin placing their objects in the correct order.

The teacher tells the children to repeat the sequence to yourself (self-talk). Take a deep breath, stop & think, then begin placing your objects in the correct order.

Variation #2:

Directions:

Tell the children to sit in a circle in a person-space pattern (a space between each person so their bodies are not touching). The teacher tells the children to focus on the persons you are sitting next to and remember "who" they are and "where" your space is in the circle.

The teacher calls out a sequence, for example, button, crayon, penny, spoon. The teacher may repeat the sequence two or three times.

When the teacher says "go" the children jog in a circle one time and return to their spaces. The children calmly sit down, take a deep breath, and place their objects from their cups in the correct order.

Remind the children to self-talk by repeating the sequence to themselves while jogging. Tell the children that jogging is slow running and that you can't pass the person in front of you.

Children have to control their impulses to jog and stay in order.

<u>Variation #3:</u>

<u>Directions:</u>

The children sit in a circle in a person-space pattern. When the teacher says, "go" the children jog, skip, or gallop around the room. They should not be in a line. Remind them to move in the same direction.

While the children are jogging the teacher calls out a sequence of objects, for example, marble, crayon, penny, button, straw. The teacher may repeat this sequence two or three times.

Remind the children to repeat this sequence to themselves while jogging to help them remember the correct order.

When the teacher says, "stop" everyone calmly returns to his or her spaces in the circle. Tell the children to sit in their **Peace** poses, take a deep breath, and then place their objects in the correct sequence from memory.

Remind the children to stop and think before they begin.

<u>Teaching Tip:</u>

Give children the opportunity to sit in their **Peace** poses and practice "self-talk" every day, saying positive thoughts to themselves.

Teachers and parents should participate with their children. It's important that children see their parents and teachers calm themselves by practicing the same methods they are teaching them to use. Remember, when teaching self-talk tell the children to:

- Say their positive words out loud for example, *"I am smart."*
- Next, tell the children to whisper these same words to themselves, *"I am smart."*
- Next, tell the children to say these words to themselves with their mouths closed (no voices).
- Repeat *"I am smart"* to yourself three times without a sound.

Self-talk is saying positive thoughts to yourself!

The teacher asks:

- How can you use self-talk to handle difficult situations?
- How do you use self-talk to help you decide what to do?
- How do you use self-talk to build confidence in yourself?

The following questions are designed to stimulate an active discussion about positive ways to handle various situations. The answers to these questions will vary from student to student.

My answers are suggestions and are written in parenthesis.

- What should you do if someone was teasing you and hurt your feelings with their words? (I would say to myself, *I will not let those words get to me. I will walk away and play with another friend*).

- What should you NOT do if someone was teasing you? (Cry or yell unkind words back to them). Why? (Because they will continue to tease you if they see their unkind words are getting to you).
- What should you do if you feel that someone was going to hurt you or someone else? (Tell an adult).
- What should you do if someone was saying hurtful things to your friend? (Stand-up for your friend by saying, my friend is a great person. Stop saying those unkind words about her).

Activity #13: Confidence & Perseverance

Materials Needed:

- A lightweight, for example a two, three, or five lb. weight depending on the age of the children.
- A timer.

Directions:

The teacher discusses confidence by asking the following question:

What is confidence?

Confidence means to believe in yourself — knowing that you have the skills to do your best, to succeed, or to work hard at something to accomplish your goals.

Confidence encourages you to try new and challenging things, understanding that it takes practice to learn a new skill and — understanding that it's ok to make a mistake.

For example,

- What do you do if you want to learn how to swim? Take lessons.
- What do you do if you want to be a good swimmer? Practice.

The more you practice, the more confident you become in yourself and your swimming. You become confident because you have learned the skills needed to become a better swimmer. You have learned the skills you need to improve your swimming or to succeed at swimming and the skills you need to work hard to accomplish your goals.

Confidence affects the way we move our bodies, the way our bodies act and feel, and the way we think. Let's practice sitting in our **Quiet & Still** poses with confidence:

- Pull your tummies up.
- Your back should be straight and your shoulders down.
- Focus straight in front of yourself.
- Breathe in your confidence! Say to yourself, *I am strong. I am confident. I believe in myself!*

Positive thoughts encourage positive choices.

Exercise #1:

The teacher asks and discusses the following questions. Suggested answers are in parenthesis.

- What is the difference between mental/emotional and physical strength? To demonstrate this concept, use a weight: two, three, or five lbs. – depending on the age of the children. Let the children lift the weight and discuss how it takes physical strength or strong muscles to lift the weight.
- Name some things we can do to build physical strength or strong muscles. (By practicing these skills that make us strong such as jogging, exercising, playing basketball, lifting weights, swimming).
- What is mental/emotional strength? (Having a strong mind/brainpower. A strong mind to control your thoughts and your body, for example, tell your body to sit quietly with your hands in your lap or tell your eyes to focus on the person who is talking).
- What kind of strength do you need to control your thoughts and your body? Mental or physical strength? (Mental strength).
- Name some ways we can build mental strength. (By practicing self-control, calming your thoughts and your body, sitting in your **Quiet & Still** or **Peace** pose and taking deep breaths. Paying attention to your body and the way your body feels).

It takes practice to build mental/emotional strength. Practicing those skills you need to control your thoughts and your body encourages impulse control. Stop & think before you act!

The teacher says, "Let's practice sitting in our **Quiet & Still** poses with confidence. Use your mental strength to control your bodies."

Tell the children you are going to set a timer for ten seconds (depending on the age of the children). Tell the children to breathe in their positive thoughts and use their mental (brainpower) strength to control their bodies. Tell your body to sit quiet & still with confidence until the timer rings.

Repeat this exercise increasing the length of time the children control their bodies by sitting in their **Peace** or **Quiet & Still** poses. I like to use a sand timer (a one, two, & three minute timer) for the children to focus on while they are sitting in their poses.

Next, tell the children to practice walking around the room with confidence — moving their bodies with good posture and form just like they were sitting in their **Quiet & Still** poses — backs straight and focusing straight in front of themselves. Children walk in the same direction.

The teacher explains that when you walk with confidence you should:

- Pull your tummies up.
- Your back should be straight and your shoulders down.
- Focus straight in front of yourself.
- Breathe in your confidence!

Exercise #2:

Materials Needed:

- Copy and print the illustrations of the following poses for the children to learn and demonstrate.

The teacher discusses perseverance by asking the following question:

What is perseverance?

Perseverance means to keep trying over and over again to accomplish your goals even when it's hard for you, such as, learning to ride a bike.

Name some other things that take practice and hard work (perseverance) to accomplish your goals.

Teach the **Tricycle** pose.

- Begin on your hands and knees.
- Take your knees off the floor and pull your tummy as far away from the floor as you can.
- Your feet should be shoulder-width apart and flat on the floor.
- Focus between your feet.
- Put one hand on top of your other hand. Your hands should be centered between your feet.
- Concentrate and balance.

Encourage students to maintain this balance for several seconds.

Teach the **Bicycle** pose (more difficult).

- Begin on your hands and knees.
- Take your knees off the floor and pull your tummy as far away from the floor as you can. Your feet should be flat on the floor.
- Your hands should be shoulder-width apart.
- Your feet should be shoulder-width apart.
- Focus on your feet.
- Put your right foot on top of your left foot. Your toes should be on top of your left foot and your heel should be resting on your left shin. Your knees should be pointing to the front.
- Put your right hand on top of your left hand.
- Your hands and feet should be in a straight line.
- Pull your tummy in tight.
- Concentrate and balance.
- Repeat on the other side.

It is challenging to balance in the **Bicycle** pose the first time it is attempted, however, with continued practice this balance can be accomplished. Encourage children to maintain their balance for several seconds.

Guide children to think about where to place their bodies and their weight to achieve this balance — the Bicycle Pose. This encourages body awareness.

Give children the opportunity to practice this pose and other poses to improve body awareness and balance. Practicing these poses encourages self-control, focus, confidence, and perseverance.

Children will frequently respond *I can't do this.* Instead tell the children to say to themselves (self-talk):

- This is hard for me.
- This is challenging.
- This is hard work.
- This pose is going to take practice.
- I'm going to keep trying until I get it (perseverance).
- Sometimes I can't do things the first time I try, but I have confidence in myself.
- I'm going to concentrate and focus on this pose.

Remind the children you can't always do something the first time you try. To learn something new you have to keep trying (perseverance) and practice.

What happens the first time you try to ride a bike? It takes practice to become better at riding your bicycle.

Ask the children:

- How can self-talk and confidence help you handle difficult situations, for example, what should you do if someone said, *I don't like what you are wearing — it's ugly.* I would say to myself, *I look great* (self-talk). *I am confident.* Then I would say out loud: *I love what I'm wearing!*
- How can you improve the skills you need to be better at:

  - Basketball
  - Dancing
  - Swimming
  - Focusing
  - Listening
  - Self-Talk
  - Self-Control

Encourage children to stop and think about the specific skills needed before they answer. For example, I can improve at basketball if I practice jumping, focusing, running, and leaping. I can improve my self-control if I practice waiting, taking deep breaths, stopping and thinking.

The teacher asks:

- How does feeling prepared build your confidence?
- What does perseverance mean?
- Why is perseverance important?
- How can perseverance help you learn the **Bicycle** pose?

Teaching Tip:

Repeat this activity by teaching and practicing other poses, such as yoga or the poses and moving balances from the book *Discover ME.*

This activity can be as hard or as easy as you need it to be depending on the poses the teacher selects and the ages of the children.

Choose poses that encourage successful experiences and build confidence. Although the poses should be challenging, children should be able to achieve them with continued practice.

It takes self-control, focus, practice, perseverance, and confidence to learn new skills!

Activity #14: What is Visualization?

Materials Needed:

- Various objects and pictures for the children to focus on, such as a ball, bubbles, a stuffed animal, a picture of a playground, the mountains, the forest, etc.

Directions:

The teacher discusses visualization by asking the following question.

What is visualization?

The teacher explains that visualization is when you use your imagination to think of what something looks like in your mind. It's creating a picture of what something looks like in your mind when you can't see it.

Exercise #1:

Tell the children to sit in the **Peace** or the **Quiet & Still** pose. Tell them to focus on each object or picture, such as a:

- Ball
- Bubbles
- Glitter Jar (p. 61)

- Cloud
- Star
- Forest

Give the children several seconds to focus on each picture or object. Next, the teacher takes the object or picture away and tells the children to visualize what they focused on and describe it. The teacher calls on the children for them to discuss their visualizations.

Exercise #2:

Directions:

Tell the children you can't see the beach right now, but you can create a picture of the beach in your mind and visualize what it looks like.

Let's describe the beach. What do you see in your imagination when you visualize what the beach looks like?

The teacher tells the children to visualize the following things. Create a picture in your mind and describe a:

- Horse
- Summer Day
- Yourself having fun or helping others

- House
- Playground
- Picnic
- Happiness

Next, tell the children to draw a picture of what they visualized those things looked like in their minds.

Exercise #3:

Materials Needed:

- The Seashore Book by Charlotte Zolotow. (Optional)

Directions:

The teacher tells the children to visualize themselves doing something that they love to do, such as baseball or dance. Ask the following questions:

- When you visualize yourself playing baseball, describe what you are doing?
- Name some things you can do to be a better baseball player.

  - Practice.
  - Watch others.
  - Use self-control.
  - Listen.
  - Focus/Concentrate.
  - Exercise to become stronger.

Visualize yourself having lots of friends. What do you see yourself doing with your friends?

Name some different ways that show friendship.

Pretend someone called you a name that wasn't nice. How can you use visualization to calm your body and your thoughts when you are feeling upset to control your actions?
Let's sit in our **Peace** poses and try it.

I visualize myself:

- Breathing and staying calm.
- Playing basketball, dancing, etc.
- Breathing in my favorite color to stay calm.
- Walking away and playing with others.
- Using self-control to keep my hands to myself.
- Being confident, I will not let those words get to me.

The teacher says, "Let's walk around the room with confidence and practice visualizing those thoughts that help us feel good about ourselves." It's fun to use calm and quiet music for the children to listen to while walking (optional).
Ask the children to share their positive thoughts they visualized.

Activity #15: Focus &Visualization

Directions:

The teacher discusses focus and visualization by asking the following question.

What do you focus on when you can't see something?

You focus on your thoughts, your imagination, your ideas, or on what you are doing.

The teacher says, "Focus on a storm. You can't see a storm right now, but you can focus on a storm and visualize or create a picture of a storm and the sound of a storm in your mind."

The teacher asks the following questions.

- What do you see when it storms?
- Is it loud or quiet?
- What do you hear when it storms?
- How does your body feel when it storms?

- What else can you tell me about the storm?
- Show me what a storm looks like with your body.
- Name some things you should do to stay safe during a storm.

Say to the children, "Focus on a monster and visualize what it looks like. The teacher asks the following questions."

- What color is it?
- Is it big or little?
- What color are the eyes?
- What shape are the eyes?
- What is it wearing?
- How does it move (use words to describe its movement)?

- Show me with your body what it looks like when it moves?
- What else can you tell me about the monster?
- Does it look happy, sad, angry, scary, or gentle? Why?

Ask the children:

How did you think of all those answers to those questions? (By focusing on your thoughts and ideas).

The teacher tells the children to draw a picture of the storm or the monster. Focus on your ideas and visualize what the storm or the monster looks like in your mind.

Stop, think, and organize your thoughts before you begin drawing. Encourage the children to create a mental image of the storm or the monster.

Remind the children to put all of their thoughts and ideas in their pictures. When the children have finished tell them this is what their thoughts, ideas, and imaginations look like.

Ask the children:

- What does it mean to "focus on your thoughts?"
- How does focusing on your positive thoughts help you control your body (your actions)?

Activity #16: Self-Control, Positive Thoughts, & Perseverance

Materials Needed:

- The Little Engine That Could by Watty Piper
- Music that's easy to walk, gallop, skip, or jog to. I like to use instrumental music.

Directions:

Read the story The Little Engine That Could by Watty Piper. Discuss with the children how the little engine used positive thoughts to succeed.

The little engine said to himself *"I think I can, I think I can,"* over and over. This story demonstrates how you can use your positive thoughts to take control of your body and — take control of the things you choose to say and do.

Choose one child to be the leader and one child to be the caboose. All the children line up in a person-space pattern and pretend to be a train. In a person-space pattern there should be a space between their bodies when standing still and when moving around the room. Tell the children to focus on the person in front of them.

Give each child something to carry such as a doll, book, etc. Turn on some music and tell the children to jog (slow running) to the music. Tell the children to whisper the following words to themselves *"I think I can, I think I can,"* over and over until the music stops.

Remind the children that it's important that each one of them cooperates with each other to complete their journey, which is to continue jogging in line while reciting their positive thoughts (*I think I can, I think I can*) until the music stops.

After the music ends continue discussing with the children how positive thoughts remind you to take control of the things you choose to say and do.

Questions to discuss:

- What are positive thoughts?
- Name some positive thoughts.
- What is self-control?
- How do positive thoughts help you to take control of your body?
- What positive thoughts did the little engine keep saying to himself?
- How did this positive thought (*I think I can*) help the little engine succeed?
- How did the little engine use self-control?
- How did the little engine use "self-talk" to stay focused?
- What is perseverance? Did the little engine have perseverance?
- Why is perseverance important?
- What is mental/emotional strength?
- How did the little engine use mental strength?
- What is the difference between mental/emotional strength and physical strength?
- Why is mental/emotional strength important?
- How can mental/emotional strength help calm your thoughts and your body?
- How can mental/emotional strength encourage positive choices?

For younger children choose a shorter piece of music so they can continue jogging until the music ends.

For older children choose a longer piece of music and let them hold something larger and heavier to make it more challenging.

Activity #17: Empathy: Velvet, Silk, & Sandpaper

Teach your students to participate in acts of kindness!

Objectives:

- To create an understanding of empathy and kindness through written and verbal communication and by participating in acts of kindness.
- To increase self-awareness — understanding, acknowledging, and identifying your feelings and also the feelings of others.
- To encourage self-control by teaching your students to take control of their thoughts and actions. Stop and think!
- To build mental and emotional strength.

Materials Needed:

- Velvet, silk, and other small pieces of soft, plush fabrics (to represent kindness).
- Sandpaper (to represent something rough). Cut several pieces into two or three inch squares.
- Copy and print the illustration of the **Peace** pose for the children to demonstrate. You may already have this pose from activity #9, peace.
- Suggested Reading (optional): The Golden Rule by Ilene Cooper.

Directions:

Italicized words are direct quotes spoken by the teacher.

The teacher says: *Have you ever thought about what your words feel like when you hear them or when you say them to others?*
Sometimes words hurt our feelings and the feelings of others. Sometimes words feel good when we hear them or when we say them to others.
How does this feel (the teacher passes around the soft, velvet, and silk fabrics for the students to touch)?

Teaching Tip:

Give students the opportunity to describe and discuss the way the fabric feels or how it makes them feel when they touch it.

This fabric is called velvet. It feels nice, soft, warm, happy, and cuddly. It feels good when we touch it. It feels good when it touches our skin.
This is what our nice, kind, and polite words feel like when we hear them or when we say them to others. Our nice and kind words feel like the way velvet and silk feels when we touch it (when it touches our skin).
Velvet and silk words feel good when we hear them or when we say them to others. Let's think of some velvet/silk words or actions we like to hear, say, and do.

Give students the opportunity to discuss velvet/silk words and actions and how velvet and silk represents kindness.

Examples of velvet/silk words and actions:

- Would you like to share my toys?
- I like your new glasses.
- Would you like to play with us?
- The picture you colored looks beautiful.
- Let's take turns.
- Thank-you for helping me clean my room.
- I'm sorry. It was an accident.

How does this feel (the teacher passes around the sandpaper for the students to touch)? You may want to tell your students to gently rub the sandpaper on the back of their hands.

Teaching Tip:

Give students the opportunity to describe and discuss the way the sandpaper feels and how it makes them feel when it touches their skin.

This is called sandpaper and it feels scratchy and rough when we touch it. This is what our mean, harsh, or angry words feel like when we hear them or when we say them to others.
Our mean, harsh, and angry words feel like the way sandpaper feels (rough & scratchy) when we touch it (when it touches our skin). Sandpaper words/actions hurt our feelings and the feelings of others when we hear them or say them.

Examples of sandpaper words and actions:

- You look funny in your glasses.
- Your dress is ugly.
- No, we don't want you to play with us.
- I don't want to help clean up.
- Ha, ha, ha, you don't know how to ride a bike!
- Pushing, shoving, not helping, not sharing, hitting, or teasing others.

Teaching Tip:

Discuss with your students velvet, silk, and sandpaper words/actions.

Show your students the illustration of the **Peace** pose. The teacher and the students sit in a circle on the floor (in a person-space pattern) in their **Peace** poses.

Peace

The teacher says to the children:

- *Sit tall and pull your tummy up. Your back should be straight and your shoulders down.*
- *Look (focus) straight in front of yourself.*
- *Your hands should be resting comfortably in your lap, palms facing up, and one hand on top of the other.*
- *Take a deep breath by breathing in the air through your nose (inhale) all the way down to your tummy and softly let the air go back out through your mouth (exhale).*
- *Control your breath. No one should hear your quiet breath except for yourself.*
- *Focus on the way your body feels.*
- *Softly breathe in (inhale) your velvet and silk words/actions. Gently blow away (exhale) the sandpaper words/actions.*
- *Take three or four deep breaths focusing on treating others like velvet (the way you would like to be treated).*

Teaching Tip:

Encourage body awareness by reminding your students to place their bodies in the correct position while sitting in the **Peace** pose.

Tell your students to focus on their bodies. The teacher asks how does your body feel when you are sitting in the **Peace** pose? For example, I feel calm, relaxed, quiet, and peaceful. I know what it feels like to be calm. This encourages the connection between the body and the mind. Our emotions are connected to our body and affect the way our body responds.

Discuss the following questions (or make up your own questions to fit the needs of your class).

The teacher asks:

How would you feel if:

- Everyone laughed at you because you kept falling off your bike? Are your friends treating you like sandpaper or velvet? How can you handle this situation?
- Your friend said, "I could help you learn to ride your bike." Is your friend treating you like sandpaper or velvet? How do you feel when someone is treating you like velvet?
- How do you feel when someone treats you like sandpaper?

How would you feel if you were being teased:

- About what you were wearing?
- Because you had an unusual name?
- Because you were wearing glasses?
- Because you were short?
- Because you had red hair?

Say to yourself: If I hear sandpaper words or if someone is treating me like sandpaper I am strong enough to:

Examples:

- Stand up for myself by looking that person in the eye and saying with confidence: stop, I don't like those words.
- Say to myself, I am an amazing person.
- Tell an adult, such as a teacher or parent.
- Say to myself, I can use my self-control to stop my body and make a positive choice. I can control my actions.
- Tell myself I am a strong and powerful person. I will not let those sandpaper words upset me.
- Say to myself, I will not let this get to me.

Think of other positive things you can do or say to yourself if someone is treating you like sandpaper.

For example, *let's all say out loud:*

- I am a wonderful person.
- I will not let sandpaper words get to me.
- I will stand up for myself.
- I will stand up for others who are being treated like sandpaper.
- I am confident in myself!
- I believe in myself!

Discuss the following statements and questions. They are designed to stimulate an active discussion about feelings and emotions.

The answers I have provided are suggestions and will vary from student to student. My answers are in parenthesis.

- When I feel mad and angry I am going to (stop and think before I decide what to do).
- When I feel upset or frustrated I am going to (take a deep breath and calm down. This helps me to make a good choice when I am feeling calm. Or I am going to calm my body by sitting and breathing in the **Peace** pose).
- What could happen if I use velvet/silk words and treat others like velvet? (Other people will be kind to me when I treat them the way I like to be treated. I will have lots of friends because I am kind and thoughtful to others).
- What could happen if I use sandpaper words and actions and treat others like sandpaper? (I will not have friends if I am unkind to others. Others will be unkind to me if I am unkind to them).
- If I see someone treating my friend like sandpaper I will (stand up for my friend).

Name and discuss some different ways (silk & velvet) that you like to be treated. Tell your students to complete this sentence:

I like my friends to be…………

Examples:

- Kind
- Thoughtful
- Respectful
- Use polite words

- Honest
- Trusting
- Encouraging
- To support me/take up for me

Say to yourself: Others like to be treated the same way I like to be treated.

Discuss the following questions (or make-up your own questions to fit the needs of your class):

- What does this sentence mean to you "the things I say and do affect the way others feel?"
- Name some ways you can control your actions when you are feeling angry.
- What is empathy? (Understanding the way others feel. Imagining how you would feel if that happened to you).
- How would you feel if your friend was crying because everyone laughed at her drawing? What would you do or say to your friend?
- What would you do or say to others who were teasing your friend? Name some ways you could help a friend who is being teased by others.
- Imagine how you would feel if you had to go to a new school where you didn't know anyone. How would you feel and how would you want others to treat you?
- How would you treat someone who is in your class that didn't know anyone?

Name and discuss some different ways (sandpaper) that you do NOT like to be treated. Tell your students to complete this sentence:

I do NOT like my friends to be…………..

Examples:

- Rude
- Mean
- Unkind

- Disrespectful
- Bossy
- Hurt me

Say to yourself: I will not treat others this way.

Discuss different ways you could show kindness at home, school, and in the community.

Exercise #1: Written Communication

Ages: 1st grade and up.
         Kindergarten (with assistance).

Directions:

(1) Students list the words they used to describe:

- Velvet & Silk Fabrics.
- Sandpaper.

(2) Give three examples of velvet & silk actions.

(3) List five ways you like to be treated. List five ways you do NOT like to be treated.

(4) Write about something kind you did for someone. Include how that person felt and how you felt about yourself.

(5) What does this sentence mean to you?

"The things I say and do affect the way others feel."

(6) Name some ways you can control your actions when you are feeling angry.

(7) What is empathy? Give an example of empathy.

(8) Name some different ways you could show kindness at home, school, or in the community.

Exercise #2: Peace & Kindness Circle

Directions:

- Begin and end your day by taking a few minutes to form a peace or kindness circle.
- Students and teachers sit in their **Peace** poses in the circle. Remind your students to place their bodies in the correct position to encourage body awareness.

- Sit tall and pull your tummy up. Your back should be straight and your shoulders down.
- Look (focus) straight in front of yourself.
- Your hands should be resting comfortably in your lap, palms facing up, and one hand on top of the other.
- Softly breathe in (inhale) your velvet and silk words/actions. Gently blow away (exhale) the sandpaper words/actions. No one should hear your quiet breath except for yourself.
- Take three or four deep breaths focusing on treating others like velvet/silk (the way you would like to be treated).
- Have your students say out loud: I am a wonderful person. I am strong and confident. I believe in myself!

Have your students come up with other positive phrases to say to themselves and out loud.

Tell your students to have a KIND DAY!

Teaching Tip: Sitting in the **Peace** pose while practicing deep breathing encourages body awareness and inspires calmness.

- *I know WHAT my body feels like to be calm, kind, and peaceful.*
- *I know HOW to control my body to be calm, kind, and peaceful.*

This exercise gives students the opportunity to practice calming their thoughts and their bodies and — controlling their actions.

Exercise #3: Kindness Reminders

- The teacher cuts soft fabric (to represent kindness) into small pieces (one inch squares). Give each student a piece of fabric to keep in their pockets to remind them to use velvet & silk words/actions with others.
- I have also given my students the opportunity to search for a small stone or rock. They cover their stones with velvet (soft fabric) using a fabric glue from an arts and crafts store. Students keep their velvet stones with them at all times to represent empathy and treating others with kindness.
- Cut a large piece of velvet (soft fabric) and place it on the classroom bulletin board to remind your class to treat others like velvet and silk.
- Cut out a large star and cover it with velvet (soft fabric) and hang it in your classroom to represent treating others with kindness.

Exercise #4: Acts of Kindness

Materials Needed:

- Index cards, one card for each person.

Directions:

Students and teachers (teachers participate in this activity) form a peace or kindness circle. Everyone sits in the circle in the **Peace** pose.

- Each student writes his or her name on an index card. You can also put a picture of each student on the index card with his or her name written on it (optional). This is helpful for the younger children.
- The teacher takes up all the cards and mixes them up.
- The teacher gives the cards back out so that each student has a card with someone else's name written on it.

Students are instructed to walk over to the person whose name is on their card and say something kind (velvet & silk words/actions) to that person.

If a person whose name they chose is talking to another student, encourage students to be patient and wait for them to finish talking before they begin.

Examples:

- Hi, would you like to sit with me at lunch today?
- Do you need some help with your math?
- Shake hands and say, good morning.
- I like your sweater.
- Thank-you for helping me clean up the classroom yesterday.

Give students the opportunity to choose a different name to say kind words to someone every day.

At the end of the week discuss with your students how it felt to be treated with kindness.

Variation: Getting to Know Each Other

Directions:

Students choose a partner by picking an index card with someone else's name written on it. Students are instructed to ask their partners various questions to get to know each other better. If necessary, the teacher may provide the questions (optional).

Examples:

- What is your first and last name?
- How old are you?
- What is your favorite food?
- Do you have a pet? If so, what kind of pet and what is his or her name?
- What is your favorite sport?
- What did you eat for breakfast this morning?
- Name your favorite animal.
- Name something you love to do.
- What is your favorite color?
- What is the name of someone in your family?
- Name something that makes you feel sad.
- Name something that makes you feel happy.

When finished the teacher asks the students what they learned and remembered about their friends by listening to each other.

Ask the students what they had in common with their friends. What were their similarities and differences?

The teacher discusses the following questions:

Why is it important:

- To listen while others are talking?
- To not interrupt others while talking?
- To always go somewhere with a friend?
- To support and stand up for your friends?
- To always let someone know where you are?

The teacher asks:

- If your friend is upset and is telling you how he or she feels, why is it important to listen to their words?

Exercise #5: Role Playing

Directions:

Describe the following scenarios (or make-up other situations to fit the needs of your class) for your students to act out. They are designed to stimulate an active discussion about empathy.

The answers I have provided are examples and will vary from student to student. My answers are in parenthesis.

Scenario #1:

You've had a great day! Your friends have treated you like silk and velvet. You've received kind words and actions all day.

Someone said, "Cool tennis shoes," as you walked by. Your teacher said, "Thank-you so much for helping me carry all these books to the classroom." You stumbled on the steps and dropped all of your papers. Someone you didn't even know asked: "Are you ok?" and helped you pick everything up. You came in third place in the swim meet that you practiced for every day, but all your friends said, "Congratulations you did a great job! You worked so hard and did your best!" You were sitting by yourself when someone asked, "Do you want to play basketball with us?" You have heard encouraging words from all of your friends.

- Describe how you feel when you hear velvet/silk words. (Happy, excited, joyful).
- Describe how your body feels when you hear velvet/silk words. (Light, relaxed, calm).
- Describe how your body would look and move when you feel good about yourself. (My face would be smiling, my eyes would be shining, I would be holding my head up and looking confident in myself. I would be walking light on my feet as if I were walking on clouds).
- Illustrate those feelings you described through the movement of your body. (Give your students the opportunity to walk around the room feeling good about themselves: smiling, excited, confident, walking loose and relaxed, etc.).

The teacher asks, "How does it feel when you are treated with kindness (silk & velvet)?"

Scenario #2:

You've had a terrible day! You've heard lots of sandpaper words and actions. You had a fight with your best friend. You tried to call and talk about it but your friend yelled: "I hate you!" Someone pointed at your hat as you walked by and shouted: "You look goofy in that hat!" Everyone began to laugh and make fun of what you were wearing. You sat all alone eating lunch as you heard people laughing at the clothes you were wearing. You tripped and dropped your books. Someone even stepped on your homework and ripped it as he pushed you aside when he ran by. You missed the winning shot in the basketball game. Your teammates shouted: "We would have won the game if you could have hit the basket. It's your fault that we lost." Everyone was ignoring you.

- Describe how you feel when you hear sandpaper words. (Sad, angry, frustrated).
- Describe how your body feels when you hear sandpaper words. (Tight, upset stomach, I clinch my jaw).
- Describe how your body would look and move when you are feeling angry, sad, or frustrated. (My face would be frowning, my eyes would be looking down at the ground, my arms would be crossed over my chest, I would be moving slow and my body would feel heavy).
- Illustrate those feelings you described through the movement of your body. (Give your students the opportunity to walk around the room feeling angry or frustrated: frowning, looking down at the ground, and moving slow and heavy).

The teacher asks, "How does it feel when you are treated unkindly (sandpaper)?"

The teacher asks the following questions:

(1) How would you treat your teammate or what would you say to him or her if they missed the winning shot in the basketball game?

(2) Your classmate wears a hearing aid. When he (or she) talks he is hard to understand. You noticed some of the kids were making fun of the way he talked. How would you treat this person who is not like you because he is wearing a hearing aid and talks differently? What would you say or do to help him feel better? What would you do or say to others who were making fun of the way he talked?

Teaching Tips:

Before your students answer the above questions remind them to:

- Stop and think!
- Imagine how you would feel if that happened to you? How would you want to be treated?
- Remember how the sandpaper felt when it touched your skin. Sandpaper words and actions can hurt your feelings and the feelings of others.
- Remember how the silk and velvet felt when it touched your skin. Silk/velvet words and actions feel good when we hear them or when we say them to others.
- Would you treat your teammate like sandpaper or would you treat him or her with silk & velvet words and actions? Why?
- Would you treat someone who speaks differently or looks differently than you like sandpaper or velvet? Why?

Remember to ask yourself:

- If I choose to do this, what could happen?
- What are the positive and negative consequences for what I choose to say and do?

The teacher says, "Let's think of some words of encouragement that help us to feel better when we hear them or when we say them to others."

Examples:

- You did a good job.
- You worked hard and tried your best.
- You never gave up.
- That took courage to stand up for your friend in front of everyone.
- We all make mistakes, but we have to keep trying.
- Believe in yourself!

Discuss the following sentence with your students:

Words are powerful, use them wisely!

Exercise #6: Kindness Journals

Ages: 1st grade and up.
    Kindergarten (with assistance).

Students keep a velvet (empathy/kindness) journal.

- Students decorate the front and back covers of their journals. My students like to cover their journals in velvet (soft fabric) to represent kindness.
- Encourage students to do at least one act of kindness every day.
- Students write about their acts of kindness and how it feels to treat others with kindness.
- Students may write about acts of kindness they received from others.
- Students write about acts of kindness they observed others doing.
- Students write in their journals at least two or three times a week.

Exercise #7: Kindness Jar

Materials Needed:

- A large clear jar.
- Pieces of fabric in various sizes, shapes, and colors.

Directions:

- Students and teachers are asked to observe acts of kindness in their home, school, classroom, and community.
- Each time an act of kindness is observed that student or teacher describes the action he or she witnessed to others while sitting in the peace or kindness circle.
- Each time a student or teacher observes an act of kindness a small piece of soft colorful fabric is placed in the kindness jar. This piece of fabric represents the act of kindness they observed.
- Use pieces of fabric in various sizes, shapes, and colors to represent diversity.
- Fill your classroom Kindness Jar with random acts of kindness! Proudly display your Kindness Jar for everyone to see.

This activity encourages awareness of your actions and the actions of others.

Teaching Tips:

Repeating these activities gives students the opportunity to practice kindness through written and verbal communication and also by participating in frequent acts of kindness.

This encourages a habit of kindness and empathy. Encourage your students to participate in acts of kindness at home, school, and in the community!

Activity #18: Listen to What Your Body is Feeling

Materials Needed:

- Shoebox
- Small cloth or towel

Directions:

Cut a hole in the top of a shoebox (large enough to put your hand inside). Fill the shoebox with various objects, such as a:

- Block
- Ball
- Marbles in a Bag (to illustrate loose)
- Carrot
- Small Opened Box
- Small Closed Box
- Feather
- Pipe Cleaner
- Sandpaper
- Weight (2 lb.)

Cover the hole with the cloth so the children cannot see what's inside the box.

Exercise #1:

The teacher says to the children, "Listen to what your body is feeling." Children take turns putting their hand inside the box to feel and manipulate one object.

Children describe the object they are feeling without seeing it, such as its shape, size, texture, weight, sound, etc.

Tell the other children to demonstrate with their bodies what the child is describing. For example, if a child is using the words round, soft, smooth, or bending to describe the object, the other children have to illustrate those words with their bodies.

Next, the teacher reminds the children to pay attention and listen to what their body is feeling. The teacher calls on one child to put his or her hand inside the box to find an object that feels smooth. The child pulls out the smooth object, for example, a block.

The teacher says everyone create a smooth movement. Listen to your body and feel your body moving smoothly. Coordinate the movement with smooth music (optional).

The teacher says describe how your body feels when you are angry, for example:

- Tight
- Heavy
- Stiff
- Rough
- Closed

The teacher calls on one child to put his or her hand inside the box to find an object that feels angry.

The child manipulates the objects inside the box to find one that represents anger, for example, the carrot feels stiff, the weight feels heavy, the sandpaper feels rough, and the box feels closed. The child pulls out the object or objects that feel angry to see and discuss those feelings.

The teacher says, "Show me what your body looks like when it's feeling angry (tight, heavy, stiff, closed)." Tell the children to hold their bodies in a tight, heavy, stiff, closed position. The teacher says, "Listen to your body and feel the anger; feel your body moving angrily." Give children the opportunity to hold their bodies in this position and move with angry feelings.

The teacher says, "Your body doesn't feel good when it's feeling tight, heavy, stiff, or closed. You are treating your body like sandpaper. Lets learn how to relax our bodies. Let's practice controlling our actions by calming our bodies down. Gently stretch and shake your body out. (Give students about one or two minutes to stretch). Let's all sit in the **Peace** pose and breathe to calm our bodies." (Give students a couple of minutes to practice taking deep breaths while sitting in the **Peace** pose and relaxing their bodies).

Describe how your body feels when you are calm and relaxed, for example,

- Loose
- Light
- Soft
- Open

The teacher calls on one person to find an object inside the box that feels calm and relaxed. After the child has found an object that feels loose (marbles), light and soft (feather), and open (opened box), take the objects out of the shoebox to see and discuss those feelings.

Say to the children, "Show me what your body looks like when it is feeling loose, light, soft, and open. Show me loose, light, and soft fingers, shoulders, legs, arms, hands, and head. Show me your whole body feeling loose, light, soft, and open."

"When your body is feeling loose, light, soft, and open you feel relaxed. Loosen, open, and relax by stretching your body. Open your shoulders and move your body with calm, relaxed feelings. Listen to the way your body feels when it's loose, calm, and relaxed. Treat your body like velvet."

Give children the opportunity to move around the room with tight, stiff, heavy bodies. Next, tell the children to relax and calm their bodies by stretching, taking deep breaths, and moving around the room feeling loose, light, and easy movements.

"It's easier to calm your body down when you listen to what your body is feeling — when you can recognize and identify the way your body feels. When you feel your body becoming angry, be nice to your body. Treat your body like velvet. Relax, breathe, loosen, and calm your body. Be kind to your body and to others."

Give children the opportunity to discuss, listen, and move to angry and peaceful music (optional). Illustrate angry movements with your body to the angry music and calm, relaxed movements to the peaceful music.

Exercise #2:

Say to the children, "Everybody has feelings and emotions. We experience lots of different feelings all day long. Every time something happens to us it makes us feel and act in lots of different ways."

Show me how your whole body looks when you are feeling:

- Happy. Finish this sentence, I feel happy when………
- Sad. I feel sad when………
  Name some things you can do to help yourself feel better.
- Surprised. Name something that surprised you.
- Serious. What does it mean to be serious? Name some things you need to be serious to do.
- Excited. What do you get excited about?
- Lonely. What is feeling lonely? Name some things you can do to help yourself not feel lonely.
- Scared. Name something that scared you. Name some things you can do to help yourself not feel afraid.
- Angry/Mad. Finish this sentence, I feel angry when………
  Name some positive things you can do when you are feeling mad to calm your body and control your actions.
- Calm/Relaxed. Finish this sentence, I feel calm and relaxed when…….
  Name some things you can do to calm your body and relax.
- Proud. What does it mean when you are feeling proud? Name some things you can do to feel proud or good about yourself.

Activity #19: Acknowledging, Recognizing, & Identifying Your Feelings

Materials Needed:

- Five or six plastic jars.
- Marbles or paper clips.

Directions:

Label jars with various emotions. You may also use pictures to designate different feelings, for example, write happy with a picture of a happy face on one jar, write angry with a picture of an angry face on another jar and write peaceful with a picture of the **Peace** pose on a jar. Other feelings you may want to label and illustrate are sad, scared, excited, frustrated, etc.

Ask the children throughout the day how they are feeling. Children drop a marble or a paper clip in the jar that represents their feelings.

Example #1: Fire drill.

Teacher: How did you feel when the fire alarm went off?
Child: Scared.
Teacher: Why were you feeling scared?
Child: It was loud.
Teacher: You are right. It is a loud noise and it does sound scary. Let's place a paper clip in the scared jar to show that you are feeling scared.
Teacher: Let's talk about and practice what's going to happen and what we are going to do next time we hear the fire alarm. We hear the loud noise to get your attention so you stop what you are doing and follow the directions to stay safe. It's important to use your self-control to organize your thoughts and your bodies to stay calm and safe.

Give children the opportunity to hear a loud noise and practice what they are supposed to do when they hear the sound of the fire alarm. The more they practice what they are supposed to do when they hear the fire alarm, the more confident they feel in themselves.

This encourages children to feel prepared to handle this challenging situation. They understand the directions and know what they are supposed to do when they hear the sound of the fire alarm.

When their scared feelings change to happy feelings, let them take the paper clip out of the scared jar and place it into the happy jar.

Teaching Tip:

This activity encourages children to acknowledge, identify, and recognize their feelings. It stimulates conversational speech by giving them the opportunity to express themselves about the way their bodies feel, such as, when asked, *how does your body feel when you are angry?*

Examples:

- My body feels tight.
- My stomach hurts.

- I grit my teeth.
- I clench my jaws.

The teacher acknowledges and identifies those feelings by saying, "You are feeling angry. Let's put a marble in the feelings jar. How are you going to calm your body and your thoughts (relax yourself) when you are feeling angry so you can control your actions?"

Examples:

- Take deep breaths.
- Watch my thoughts settle while focusing on the glitter jar (p. 61).

The teacher says, "You have calmed your thoughts and your body. Let's put the marble in the "peaceful" jar."

Understanding your body and verbalizing your thoughts and feelings encourages self-awareness. This inspires children to acknowledge and discuss their feelings, but control their actions.

Children learn that they experience many different feelings throughout the day and that they also have the skills and strategies they need to control their behavior (actions).

Children learn positive ways to handle their feelings/emotions. Giving children the opportunity to practice those skills and strategies they need to control their impulses encourages competency in those skills.

This inspires confidence in yourself — knowing that you have the necessary skills to safely get through a challenging situation.

Example #2:

Teacher: Why are you crying?
Child: Because they won't let me play with them.
Teacher: I can see you are feeling sad. Let's put a paper clip in the sad jar to show how you are feeling.
Teacher: How were they treating you?
Child: Like sandpaper. They won't let me play with them.
Teacher: How do you feel when you are treated this way? Sad.
Teacher: Name some things you like to do that make you feel happy.
Child: Color, play with dolls.
Teacher: Let's try doing some of those things.
Teacher: How do you feel? Happy.
Teacher: Let's take the paper clip out of the sad jar and place it in the happy jar to show that now you are feeling happy.

Empower children with the skills needed to handle challenging situations. This encourages confidence; children feel prepared and they know what they are supposed to do.

Children understand that they have choices and that their choices affect the outcome of a situation.

Activity #20: Focus & Concentration

Materials Needed:

- Copy and print the illustration of the **Bridge** pose for your students to focus on.

Directions:

The teacher says to the children, "Focus on the **Bridge** pose. (Show the picture of the **Bridge** pose). Focus on or look at the placement of the feet, hands, head, eyes, legs, and whole body." After a few seconds the teacher takes the picture away.

The teacher says, "Visualize the **Bridge** pose. Think about what the pose looks like inside your mind, even though you are not looking at it. Remember where to place your body. Remember what the pose looks like and balance in the **Bridge** pose."

Before balancing in the **Bridge** pose remind the children to:

- Take a deep breath.
- Stop and think.
- Focus on your body. Ask the children, "How do you focus or concentrate on your body without looking at it?" (By thinking about the way your body feels and moves in your thoughts).
- Ask yourself, *how should I move my body to create the **Bridge** pose* (self-talk)? Slow, smooth, and quiet.
- Say to yourself, *I can do this* (self-talk).

For younger children, the pose does not have to be perfect. The goal is to encourage and experience self-control and focus through body awareness.

Bridge

Ask the following questions:

- How did you learn this pose? (By focusing and concentrating on the pose).
- Why is it important to focus on what you are doing?
- How did you organize your thoughts to help you remember where to place your body in the **Bridge** pose?
- How did self-control help you to learn this pose?
- Name some ways you can use self-control (controlling the things you say & do) in the classroom and at home.

Repeat this activity using different poses to focus on, such as yoga or the poses and moving balances from the book *Discover ME*.

Activity #21: Breathing

Materials Needed:

- Copy and print the illustration of the **Relax** pose.
- Lightweight block or paper plate.

Directions:

You can use the lightweight block, paper plate, or your hands for this activity.

Exercise #1:

The teacher explains to the children that self-control is being in charge of your own body. "Let's practice the **Relax** pose." (Show the picture of the **Relax** pose).

If you are using the block tell the children to place it on top of their tummies while resting in this pose.

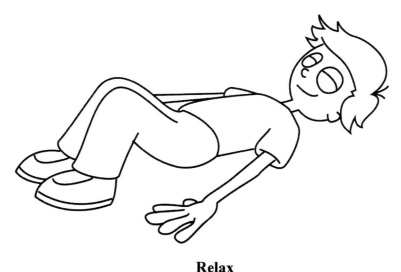

Relax

Tell the children to take a deep breath all the way down to their tummies. When they breathe in they will see the block go up on their tummies and when they breathe out they will see the block come down.

The teacher says to the children, "Take a deep breath by breathing in the air through your nose (inhale) all the way down to your tummy and gently blow the air back out through your mouth (exhale). Control your breath. You are the only person who should hear the sound of your quiet breath."

Next, tell the children to close their eyes, breathe, and feel the block on their tummies move up and down as they breathe in and out. Remind the children to breathe in a long, slow, steady stream of air into their bodies all the way down to their tummies.

Next, the teacher tells the children to take the blocks off their tummies. Imagine your tummy is a balloon and you are filling it up with air when you breathe in. When you gently blow all of the air out, your tummy becomes flat like a balloon.

This exercise encourages children to visualize and create a mental image of deep breathing.

While the children are relaxing in their poses the teacher says:

I know what it looks like to breathe and relax. I know what it feels like to breathe and relax. I know how to breathe deeply to calm my thoughts and my body. I know what it feels like to make my body stop and think before I decide what to do.

Teaching Tip:

Discuss with the children how their bodies feel after practicing the **Relax** pose and breathing. Talk about how taking deep breaths and relaxing helps to calm your thoughts and your body (your actions). It gives you the time you need to stop your body and think of some positive choices you should do before you act. Encourage children to organize their thoughts and their actions.

Repeat this exercise without using the block on their tummies. Tell the children to close their eyes and focus on their breathing and the way their bodies feel when they are calm and relaxed.

Remind the children what it means to focus by asking,

- What do you focus on when you can't see something?
- What is self-control?
- How do you organize your body and your thoughts to calm down?

Exercise #2:

Directions:

The teacher says pretend someone is teasing you by calling you a name that hurts your feelings. How can you handle this situation?

During this discussion encourage the children to talk about how self-control, focus, organizing their thoughts and actions, visualizations, and confidence can make it easier to handle difficult situations.

Ask the following questions:

- What is confidence?
- Why is it important to move or walk with strength, courage, and confidence?

Name some different ways you could build strength, courage, and confidence in yourself.

Suggestions:

- Be prepared.
- Know what you are going to do when you are in a difficult situation.
- Know how to organize your thoughts and your actions to stay calm so you can make a positive choice.
- Stop and think before you say or do something.
- Practice all of the above ideas so you know what to do and how to control your actions in challenging situations.

The teacher tells the children to practice calming their thoughts and their bodies while walking. Remember to walk with self-control and focus — walk with strength, courage, and confidence. You should walk with good posture — back straight, shoulders down, head up, and focus on your surroundings.

Next, tell the children to jog (slow, controlled running). While jogging tell the children to visualize themselves doing something that makes them feel good about themselves or something that makes them feel happy.

After completing this exercise discuss with the children what they visualized that made them feel good about themselves.

Activity #22: Consequences

If I choose to do this, what could happen? Students learn that there are positive and negative consequences for the choices they make.

Directions:

The teacher says to the children, "Pay attention means to stop, look, and listen. Stop your body, look at the person who is talking, and listen to the spoken words (hear & remember). It takes self-control to pay attention."

Exercise #1:

The teacher says, "Let's practice paying attention."

- Pay attention to me. When the teacher has their attention — bodies still, eye contact, and they are listening to the person talking — the teacher gives a direction. For example, clap your hands, shake your hands, or stop moving your hands.
- Pay attention to (call the name of someone else in the room). What color is her shirt?
- Pay attention to (call the name of someone else in the room). Ask that person to give a direction for the other students to follow.

"You know how to pay attention. You know how to stop, look, and listen to the person who is talking."
"Pay attention to me." The teacher asks the following questions:

- What are consequences? Consequences are when you say to yourself, *if I choose to do this, what could happen?* Or what comes next? Those are the consequences. For example, if you choose to leave your bike outside in the front yard overnight, what could happen? It could get stolen or if it storms it could be damaged. Those are the consequences for leaving your bike outside. Those are negative (bad) consequences.
- What if you choose to put your bike away? What could happen? Your bike will be safe. That is a positive (good) consequence.
- What should you do before you make a choice? Stop and think about the consequences for what you choose to say and do. Then choose a positive way to handle it.
- Encourage children to practice asking themselves this question, *if I choose to do this, what could happen?*

Teaching Tip:

Discuss with your students the importance of "paying attention" to yourself — the things you choose to say and do and the importance of paying attention to others — the things they choose to say and do.
This increases self-awareness and also encourages awareness of other people's actions and feelings.

<u>Exercise #2:</u>

<u>Materials Needed:</u>

- Masking Tape

<u>Directions:</u>

Children stand in a horizontal line next to each other (a space between their bodies). Each child stands on a piece of masking tape. If you have ten children you will need ten pieces of tape in a row for each child to stand on.

Put another piece of tape directly across from those pieces on the opposite side of the room. Place the pieces of tape far enough away from each other so the children have room to jog back and forth from one piece of tape to the other.

Tell the children to stand on the masking tape and pay attention (to the teacher). Stop, look, and listen to the person talking.

When the teacher has their attention: bodies still, eye contact, and ready to listen—the teacher gives the following directions.

- When I say "go" jog towards the other piece of masking tape.
- You have to control your body and stop on top of the piece of tape. Stop on your feet.
- You cannot pass the tape.
- When you get to the tape, calm your body down as quickly as you can and pay attention (stop, look, & listen) to the teacher.

The children jog back and forth (no voices) from tape to tape. Each time they get to the piece of tape, they pay attention (stop, look, & listen) to the teacher and wait patiently for their name to be called to answer a question.

Remind your students to ask themselves, *what are the positive and negative consequences for what I choose to say and do?*

Always adapt the questions to fit the needs of your students.

Sample Questions:

- What are the positive consequences for brushing your teeth?
- What are the negative consequences for not brushing your teeth?
- What are the positive consequences for using self-control?
- What are the negative consequences for not using self-control?
- What are the positive consequences for exercising?
- What are the negative consequences for not exercising?
- What are the positive consequences for calming your thoughts and your body before you make a choice?
- What are the negative consequences for not calming your thoughts and your body before you make a choice?
- It's time to eat dinner. Stop and think! What do you do before you eat? What are the positive consequences for washing your hands?
- What are the negative consequences for not washing your hands?

- What does it mean to organize your thoughts?
- What are the positive consequences for organizing your thoughts?
- What are the negative consequences for not organizing your thoughts?
- What are the positive consequences for studying for your test?
- What are the negative consequences for not studying for your test?
- It's time to go to bed. Stop and think! What are the positive consequences for getting a good night's sleep?
- What are the negative consequences for staying up late and not getting enough sleep?
- What are the positive consequences for being kind and thoughtful to others?
- What are the negative consequences for being thoughtless, rude, and unkind?
- What would you do if someone were teasing your friend? Why?
- Someone pushed you down. Ask yourself, if I push him back what could happen next? Or if I don't push him back what could happen?
- What are the positive consequences for stopping and thinking before you decide what to do?
- What are the negative consequences for not stopping and thinking before you decide what to do?
- You needed a ride home from the party, but you know the person who is driving has been drinking. What are the negative consequences for getting into the car with someone who has been drinking? What are the positive consequences for not getting into the car?
- You know someone who is being bullied. What are the positive consequences for helping that person by supporting him or her and telling an adult? What are the negative consequences for not helping that person or not telling an adult? Imagine how you would feel if you were that person who was being bullied and needed help.

Teaching Tip:

This is empowering for children and adults when they realize that they have control over their own lives by the choices they make, understanding that their choices affect the outcome of a situation.

Discuss the following questions with your students:

What does it mean to pay attention to others?

- To think about the way you treat others.
- To think about the way others feel.

What does it mean to pay attention to yourself?

- To think about the way your body feels.
- To think about the way your body is acting.
- To focus on your thoughts.
- To think about the way you treat others.

Teaching Tip:

How do you prepare yourself to become competent using self-control and handling challenging situations? Practice.

Children need to be given the opportunity to role-play and discuss how they plan to handle various situations before they occur.

The key to self-control is practice! Practice encourages competence! Competence encourages confidence!

- Stop and think about the consequences (positive and negative) for what you choose to say and do.
- Ask yourself, *if I choose to do this, what could happen?*
- Make a positive choice to encourage a positive outcome.
- Remember you have self-control. Take charge of the situation with strength, courage, and confidence.
- Believe in yourself!

Activity #23: Listening

Materials Needed:

- Bells – two or three bells that sound different, but similar.
- Maraca.
- Drum.
- Sandshaker – tape two paper cups together with sand inside.
- Riceshaker – tape two paper cups together with rice inside.
- Beanbag.
- Marbles in a can.
- Tambourine.
- Pencil to tap on the desk or floor.

Directions:

The teacher explains that listening means to hear and remember. Tell the children to focus on the various objects (from the above list). Listen and remember the sound each object makes.

The teacher repeatedly shakes each object he or she is using. Students focus on the object, listen, and remember the sound of each object. Students identify the object by the sound it makes.

Give children the opportunity to hear the sound of each object numerous times, while they are focusing on it, to encourage them to remember which object is making which sounds.

For example, the teacher shakes an object (the red bell) and asks, "What is the name of the object that is making this sound?" Children wait for their names to be called before they answer.

Exercise #1:

Tell the children to get into the **Relax** pose and close their eyes.

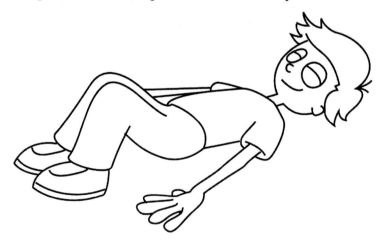

The teacher shakes one object at a time. He or she then calls on one person to identify which object made that sound. Students listen, focus, and concentrate on the sounds they hear. Children have to listen carefully to determine which object is making the sound they hear without seeing it.

The similar the sounds, the harder it is to identify the object or instrument. For example, children have to focus and concentrate to determine if the sound they hear is coming from the sandshaker, the riceshaker, or the beanbag.

After the children have practiced their listening skills discuss how they used focus, concentration, and self-control to listen to the sound and identify the object.

Repeat this activity by using different musical instruments and objects. The similarity of the sounds increases the difficulty of the task.

Exercise #2:

Materials Needed:

- Select a piece of slow, gentle, and calm instrumental music.
- Copy and print the illustrations of the poses on the following pages for the children to demonstrate.

Directions:

Play a piece of quiet, smooth, and slow music for the children to listen to. Ask the following questions:

- Can you see the music? (No)
- Can you hear the music? (Yes)

Tell the children to focus on the music. The teacher asks, "What do you focus on when you can't see the music? You focus on the way the music sounds."

Tell the children to describe the way the music sounds or moves, for example, I hear slow, quiet, smooth, gentle, or soft music.

The teacher tells the children to move their bodies to the sound of the music. Control your body by moving it the way the music sounds (gentle, slow, soft, etc.).

Next, the teacher calls out the directions on the following pages for the children to demonstrate.

The teacher says:

- Move your body to the sound of the music (about 30 seconds).
- **Put Your Body Back Together**. Stop your body. Place your hands by your sides. Glue your feet together. Take a deep breath. (Hold this pose for a few seconds).

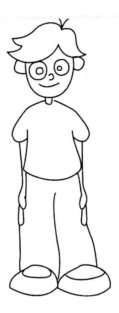

- Move your body to the sound of the music.
- Stop your body. Stretch your hands above your head. **Reach For the Stars** (hold this position for a few seconds).

- Slowly bring one arm down by your side. Slowly bring your other arm down by your side. Take a deep breath.
- Move your body to the sound of the music.
- Stop your body. Stand in your **Quiet & Still** pose (hold this position for a few seconds). Take a deep breath.

- Move your body to the sound of the music.
- Stop your body. **Open**. Open your feet (with a medium space between them). Open your arms out to the sides of your body. Reach and stretch (hold this position for a few seconds).

- Glue your feet together. Glue your arms to your sides. Take a deep breath.
- Open your feet (with a medium space between them). Open your arms out to the sides of your body. Reach and stretch (hold this position for a few seconds).
- Gently and slowly turn your body around one time and **Reach For the Stars** (hold this position for a few seconds).
- Gently and slowly turn your body around the opposite direction one time and **Reach For the Stars** (hold this position for a few seconds).
- Slowly bring one arm down by your side. Slowly bring your other arm down by your side. Glue your feet together.
- Take a deep breath.

Repeat this sequence once or twice. Describe the children's actions with the appropriate language to encourage children to create a mental image of self-control and to increase their understanding of this abstract concept. *I know what self-control looks like. I know what it feels like to have self-control. I know what it feels like to take control of my body.*

Examples of descriptive language:

- You are moving your body to the sound of the music. That takes self-control to make your body move slowly.
- You are focusing on the way the music moves. Your body is jogging slowly, quietly, and smoothly just like the sound of the music. You are in charge of the way your body moves. You have self-control.
- That takes a lot of self-control to balance in your **Quiet & Still** pose without moving.
- When you breathe you are taking in a slow, long, steady stream of air all the way down to your tummy. That takes patience and self-control to calm your body down and relax. You are responsible for what your body does. You know how to calm yourself (your body) down.

The teacher asks the children:

- How did you use self-control to make yourself listen?
- Why is it important to listen to yourself and to others?

Repeat this activity by choosing music with various rhythms and tempos for the children to listen to, describe, move their bodies to then — stop and balance in a pose.

Activity #24: STAR

Materials Needed:

- Star Stencil. Print and cut out enough stars for each student.

Exercise #1:

Providing a visual reminder encourages children to stop and think before they act.

Directions:

Each child decorates or colors a star. Write the word "STAR" on or above their pictures and discuss with the children what the "STAR" represents.

S - Stop & think.
T - Take a deep breath — take responsibility for your thoughts and actions.
A - Ask yourself: *If I choose to do this, what could happen?*
R - Resolve the conflict peacefully.

Place the stars in a visible place in your classroom to consistently remind your students the importance of what their STAR represents.

Have your students take "star breaks" during the day. Tell them to sit in the **Peace** pose and take deep breaths. This reinforces the connection between the body and mind by giving them the opportunity to practice calming their thoughts and their bodies.

While sitting in their **Peace** poses encourage your students to visualize a STAR, what it represents and — how this can help you make positive choices.

When your class becomes to loud and active just point to your classroom stars. This immediately reminds the children to stop and think.

Give children the opportunity to practice this formula on a daily basis to encourage the development of this technique to handle challenging situations. Their STAR reminds them to practice self-control. Stop and think before you act!

Remind the children to say to themselves (self-talk):

When I see my star or when I think about (visualize) the stars it reminds me to calm down. It reminds me to say to myself, I am a STAR. I know how to stop, think, and make a positive choice.

Remember to ask yourself, *if I choose to do this, what could happen?* This encourages children to stop and think about the positive and negative consequences for what they choose to say and do.

The following paragraph is an example of using descriptive language to encourage children to visualize and understand their feelings.

The teacher says:

I can see you are feeling upset because your friend said you couldn't play with them. Those sandpaper words hurt your feelings. Let's take a STAR break and let your feelings settle and calm down so you can think clearly before you decide what to do.

Exercise #2:

Students use the STAR formula to role-play and handle the following situations. Discuss with your students the positive and negative consequences for what they choose to say and do and how their choices can influence a positive or a negative outcome.

Scenarios:

- You are playing basketball and two older kids take the ball away from you.
- A stranger said, "I want to show you some puppies. They are in my car. Come with me and I'll show you."
- Some kids are encouraging you to take something out of someone else's backpack.
- You see a group of kids teasing and making fun of one of your friends.

Teaching Tips:

- Children need to understand and acknowledge their feelings, but learn how to control their actions.
- You can control the things you say and do — how you choose to deal with various situations.
- The things you say and do are a choice.
- When children gain experience controlling their thoughts and actions by responding to their emotions in a positive way, they begin to understand that they have the ability to control themselves and their lives. This encourages confidence — believing in yourself! This is empowering for children and adults when they realize that they have control over their own lives by the choices they make — understanding that their choices affect the outcome of a situation.
- Self-control! Give children the skills and strategies they need to control their impulses!

Exercise #3:

Materials Needed:

- Copy and print the illustrations of the following poses for the children to learn and demonstrate.

Directions:

- Teach the following star poses.

Relaxing Star

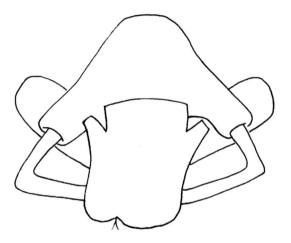

- Sit with your legs crisscrossed.

Twinkling Star

- Gently and slowly wiggle your fingers and shoulders.
- Concentrate on keeping your lower body still.

Rising Star

When rising to a standing position your arms stay crossed over your chest.

- Uncross your legs and gently roll up to your knees. Pull your tummy up (do not sit back on your heels).
- Balance on both of your knees. Keep your tummy pulled up and your shoulders down.
- Place one foot on the floor in front of you and balance (hold for several seconds). Change and balance with your other foot in front.
- Pull your body up to a standing position.
- Cross your feet (slightly bend your knees).
- Balance, breathe, and twinkle — gently and slowly wiggle your fingers and shoulders.
- Concentrate on keeping your lower body still.
- Stop twinkling and take a deep breath.
- Move your hands away from your chest.
- Arms stay crossed, fingers point down and your palms come together, fingers begin to point upward and your hands move above your head.
- Hold and balance in your **Rising Star** pose with confidence.

Repeat the star sequence:

- **Relaxing Star** pose – Stay in this position and relax for several seconds and breathe.
- Take a deep breath (inhale) while lifting your upper body into the **Twinkling Star** pose and exhale.
- **Rising Star** pose.

Reverse the star sequence:

- **Rising Star**
- **Twinkling Star**
- **Relaxing Star**

This sequence should be a smooth transition when moving your body from one pose to another.

Visualization — tell the children to visualize their stars rising high in the sky with confidence. The teacher reads the following sentences while the children are balancing and demonstrating the star sequence.

The stars relax and rest (relaxing star pose) *until the sun sets. When the sun sets the stars awaken and begin to twinkle* (twinkling star pose). *The stars rise high in the sky* (rising star pose) *and proudly shine with strength, courage, and confidence.*

Tell the children to say to themselves, *I am a STAR.* Children should hold this pose for several seconds.

Reverse this sequence and finish in the **Relaxing Star** pose.

The teacher asks the following question:

What does your STAR represent? Or what does your STAR remind you to do?

Encourage both children and adults to control their impulses by visualizing a STAR and what it represents.

S - Stop & think before you act.
T - Take a deep breath — take responsibility for your thoughts and actions.
A - Ask yourself: *If I choose to do this, what could happen? What are the positive and negative consequences for what I choose to say and do?*
R - Resolve the conflict peacefully.

<u>Teaching Tip:</u>

- Self-control is learned just like you learn to read, write, or do math. It takes time to develop self-control and lots of practice to use it effectively to control your behavior.
- Remind your students to visualize their STAR and what it represents before they make a choice.
- Competency in the skills and strategies needed to handle life's many challenges encourages self-confidence. Confidence encourages children to trust and believe in themselves!

Activity #25: Focus, Concentration, & Visualization

Directions:

The teacher says to the children, "We think, pay attention, and focus on things we cannot see. Concentration is focusing and paying attention to your thoughts, your imagination, and your ideas."

Exercise #1:

Tell the children to focus and concentrate on a cloud. Visualize and concentrate on what the cloud looks like in your mind.

The teacher asks the following questions for the children to discuss:

- What shape is your cloud?
- Does it look happy, sad, angry, or scary? Why?
- What color is it?
- Sometimes a cloud looks like an animal or an object. What does your cloud look like?
- What's floating on top of your cloud and underneath it?
- If you had your very own cloud, what would you use it for?
- Tell me how your cloud moves across the sky.
- Show me with your body how your cloud moves across the sky.

Exercise #2:

Directions:

The teacher says, "Pretend you own a pair of magic shoes. Focus on your magic shoes and visualize what they look like and what they can do."

The teacher asks the following questions (optional):

- What color or colors are your magic shoes?
- What kind of shoes are they?
- Describe what they look like.
- What kind of powers do your shoes have?
- What happens when you wear them?
- What happens when you take them off?

Focus and concentrate on your magic shoes. Visualize, describe, and write a story about how you use your magic shoes to create acts of kindness. Draw pictures to illustrate your story.

Teaching Tip:

Encourage the children to create mental images of their thoughts. Remind them to organize all of their ideas and put them in their pictures. When they have finished, tell them this is what their thoughts and ideas look like.

Ask the children:

How did you think of so many interesting ideas? (By focusing and concentrating on my imagination and thoughts. Visualizing and organizing my ideas).

Other ideas to visualize, describe, and draw:

- The Forest
- A Winter's Day
- Yourself

- Self-Control
- Your Family
- How to Calm Down

<u>Activity #26:</u> <u>Breathing: Learning How to Control My Actions by Calming My Thoughts & My Body</u>

<u>Materials Needed:</u>

- Small soft sponges. Each person gets two sponges.

<u>Directions:</u>

Tell the children to get into the **Relax** pose — close their eyes and focus and concentrate on their bodies.

The teacher asks, "How do you focus on your body without looking at it?" (By concentrating on the way your body feels and moves).

Relax

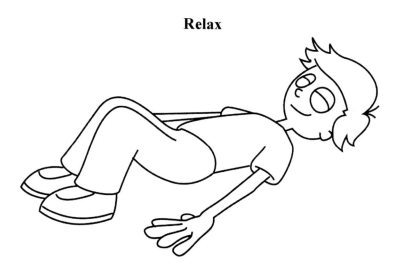

Give the children a small sponge to hold in each hand. The teacher says to the children:

"Clench or squeeze the sponges by tensing the muscles in your hands as tight as you can. Tighten or tense your muscles by using the energy in your hands to squeeze the sponges and hold them till I count to four. (The teacher counts out loud). Gently release and relax your hands. Slowly open your hands and gently stretch your fingers. Slowly wiggle your fingers."

Repeat this exercise by squeezing the sponge and releasing it in one hand, then the other hand.

Next, the teacher takes the sponges away and tells the children to tense the muscles in their hands by curling them into tight fists. Children tense their muscles and hold for several seconds (while the teacher counts to either four or eight) before telling them to release and relax their muscles by uncurling their fists and stretching their hands.

Follow this same format giving the children time to tense and release the muscles in their arms, feet, legs, and whole body.

The teacher tells the children to keep their eyes closed and — focus and think about the movement of your:

- Hands – slowly circle your hands around and around (a few seconds). Stop your hands. Clench your hands into tight fists (hold for a few seconds). Slowly open your hands and stretch your fingers long. Slowly wiggle your fingers.
- Feet – Slowly extend your legs straight out in front of you (do not arch your back). Slowly circle your feet around and around (a few seconds). Stop your feet. Curl your toes in and clench your feet tight (hold a few seconds). Slowly uncurl your toes and stretch your feet. Alternate pointing and flexing (toes point towards the ceiling) your feet.
- Relax your whole body by letting go of all the tension.
- Breathe – Concentrate on keeping your body quiet, still, and feeling calm and relaxed. Take a deep breath by breathing in the air through your nose (inhale) all the way down to your tummy and softly let the air go back out through your mouth (exhale). Control your breath. No one should hear your quiet breath except for yourself.
- Lift one leg up. Hold it up while I count to four (the teacher counts out loud). Bring your leg down gently.
- Lift your other leg up. Hold it up while I count to four (the teacher counts out loud). Bring your leg down gently.
- Relax, take deep breaths, and concentrate on letting go of all the tension in your body. Focus and concentrate on the way your body feels (calm & relaxed).

Exercise #2:

Materials Needed:

- Maraca
- Bell

Directions:

While resting in the **Relax** pose tell the children to focus on the sound of the maraca and the sound of the bell.

When the teacher gently shakes the maraca tell the children to take a deep breath in through their noses (inhale) all the way down to their tummies to the sound of the maraca. When the teacher quietly shakes the bell tell them to gently blow all of the air out through their mouths (exhale) to the sound of the bell.

The teacher tells the children to relax while they take one or two deep breaths. Tell them to focus and concentrate on coordinating their breath by inhaling to the sound of the maraca and exhaling to the sound of the bell.

Teaching Tip:

Discuss with the children how they can use these breathing techniques to calm their thoughts and their bodies when they are feeling angry, upset, or frustrated.

Exercise #3:

Materials Needed:

- Masking Tape
- Drum
- Tambourine

- Picture of a Flower
- Maraca
- Bell

Suggested Reading: The Listening Walk by Paul Showers (optional)

Directions:

The teacher places pieces of masking tape randomly around the room. Each child stands on a piece of tape. Tell the children to focus on the teacher to WATCH and LISTEN for the directions.

- When the teacher taps the drum, children move around the room to the beat.
- When the teacher shakes the tambourine, children calmly return to their tape and move in place to the sound of the tambourine.
- When the teacher holds up the picture of a flower, children calm their bodies by sitting in the **Quiet & Still** or **Peace** pose on their piece of tape. Children place their bodies on the floor without a sound.
- When children hear the sound of the maraca they take a deep breath in through their noses (inhale) and when they hear the sound of the bell they gently blow the air back out through their mouths (exhale).

Children continue to listen and focus on the teacher while moving their bodies and sitting in their poses to WATCH and LISTEN for the directions. When moving around the room children should always move in the same direction.

Remind the children what they are supposed to do when they hear or see the objects:

- Drum – Move around the room. The teacher may call out various ways for the children to move to the beat, such as jogging, skipping, dancing, walking, galloping, etc.
- Tambourine – Return to your tape and continue moving in place.
- Flower – Sit on your tape in your **Quiet & Still** or **Peace** pose.
- Maraca – Take a deep breath. Breathe in (inhale) to the sound of the maraca.
- Bell – Gently breathe out (exhale) to the sound of the bell.

Tell the children to repeat the directions to themselves to help them remember what they are supposed to do (self-talk).

Repeat this activity by presenting different objects for the children to focus on and listen to.

Activity #27: Self-Control

Directions:

The teacher says to the children, "Self-control is being in charge of your own body and being able to control it." It is being able to control your hands, feet, shoulders, arms, legs, head, voices and — your whole body. Self-control is being able to control your thoughts and actions.

The teacher calls out the following directions for the children to demonstrate with no voices.

- Clap your hands loudly. Clap your hands softly.
- Put your hands above your head.
- Shake your hands as fast as you can.
- Move your arms and your hands as slowly as you can.
- Put your hands behind your back.
- Stamp your feet loudly. Stamp your feet quietly.
- Run in place.
- Take a body break. Stand in your **Quiet & Still** pose and take deep breaths. Keep your body quiet and still. (The teacher should let them maintain this pose for several seconds before giving the next direction).
- Put one hand up and one hand down.
- Walk around the room quietly. Walk around the room noisily.
- Calm your body. Sit in your **Quiet & Still** pose and take deep breaths. Make your body stop moving. (Children hold their poses for several seconds).
- Make your body jump up and down noisily. Make your body jump up and down quietly.
- Wiggle one leg.
- Reach both hands to the side of your body.
- Put one hand above your knee and the other hand below your knee.
- Wiggle your whole body.

- Calm your whole body by sitting in the **Peace** pose. Take charge of your body. Make your body stop moving, calm down, and practice breathing. (Children hold this pose for several seconds).
- Run fast. Stop.
- Jump up and down while saying your ABC's.
- Walk as if you are feeling proud of yourself. Pick your tummy up. Your back should be straight and your shoulders down.
- Walk with a slouched, messy body. Drop your tummy & your back.
- Walk with confidence (good posture).
- Shake your whole body all around.
- Take a body break. Show me how quickly you can calm your body. Stop your body and sit in your **Quiet & Still** pose. Breathe. (Hold this pose for several seconds).
- Walk as if your body is feeling calm, relaxed, & loose.
- Walk as if your body is feeling tense, tight, & stressed.
- Take a body break. Sit in your **Quiet & Still** pose and breathe. (Hold this pose for several seconds). Visualize yourself floating on a cloud.

The teacher asks the following questions:

(1) How do you use self-control:

- To calm your body down?
- To control your actions when you are feeling mad, upset, frustrated, or angry?
- On the playground?
- In the classroom?
- When you are playing with a group of friends?
- When someone hurts your feelings?

(2) What could happen if you didn't use self-control?

(3) Why is self-control important?

Teaching Tip:

This activity gives your students the opportunity to practice moving their bodies from a hyper state to calming their bodies down.

Children need to be given the opportunity to calm themselves down by taking control of their bodies by focusing and concentrating on their thoughts and actions.

Repeat this activity by creating your own movement combinations for your students to practice moving their bodies from a hyper state to being quiet and still.

Remember, the more opportunities children are given to practice controlling their actions by taking the responsibility to calm their bodies down, the more competent they become at controlling their impulses.

Activity #28: Self-Control & Breathing

Materials Needed:

- Bell
- Copy and print the following poses for your students to learn and practice.

Directions:

The teacher says to the children, "Self-control is being in charge of your own body. Use your positive thoughts to tell your body to calm down, relax, and breathe."

Have your students take a body break by stopping what they are doing and listening to the way their bodies feel — focusing and concentrating on their thoughts, their bodies, and their breathing.

Tell them to take a body break by breathing, calming their bodies down, and resting their bodies in the following poses.

Children should stay in each pose and hold that position for several seconds before demonstrating the next pose. Tell the children to hold each pose until they hear the sound of the soft bell.

Each time the teacher rings the bell the children quietly change poses. It should be a smooth transition when changing your body from one pose to another.

Exercise #1:

Teach your students the following poses. After the children have learned the poses, the teacher can call out the name of the pose or show the picture of the pose for the students to demonstrate.

The teacher tells the children to tune out everything around them. Focus and concentrate on the following words: quiet, still, and calm. Repeat these words to yourself to remind your body to stay quiet, still, and calm. Encourage your body to listen (connect) to your positive thoughts.

The teacher says, "Let's begin by resting in the **Relax** pose." Remind the children to stay in each pose until they hear the sound of the quiet bell before they gently move their bodies into the next pose.

Relax

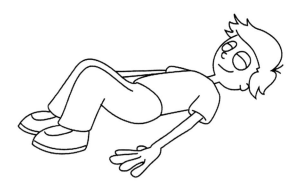

Peace

Circle of Peace

Giving Peace

Relaxing Star

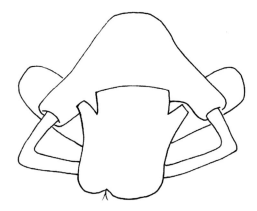

Elevator Up

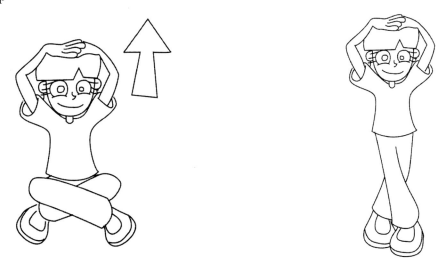

- Slowly & smoothly rise to a standing position (keeping your hands on your head).

Twinkling Star

- Gently and slowly wiggle your fingers and your shoulders.
- Concentrate on keeping your lower body still.

Rising Star

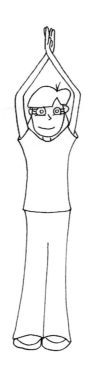

Put Your Body Back Together

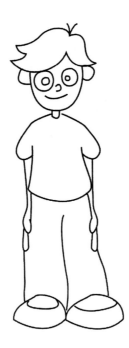

Elevator Down

- Slowly and smoothly lower your body to the floor (keeping your hands on your head) to a sitting position (legs remain criss-crossed).

Quiet & Still - Sitting

Give children the opportunity to learn this movement and breathing sequence by practicing daily.

Discuss with the children what self-control feels like and looks like. Select peaceful background music (optional) and tell the children to relax and calm their bodies in their poses while listening to the music.

Ask the following questions:

- Which pose is your favorite? Why?
- What positive thoughts were you thinking?
- How do your positive thoughts help you to calm your body? How do your positive thoughts help you to control your actions?
- How does your body feel when you are resting and being calm in your poses?
- How does a body break help you to calm down?

Teaching Tip:

Encourage children to take body breaks throughout the day by breathing and practicing these poses. A body break gives you the time you need to stop and think.

Exercise #2:

Take pictures of the children practicing their poses. This gives children the opportunity to see themselves being calm and peaceful using self-control.

Exercise #3:

Tell the children to choose a pose and visualize themselves in that pose. Next, tell the children to focus on themselves practicing that pose in their minds. This encourages children to organize their thoughts and ideas (mental planning).

Next, tell the children to draw a picture of themselves demonstrating that pose from memory.

Activity #29: Cooperation

Materials Needed:

- Large pieces of drawing paper.
- Crayons or markers.

Directions:

The teacher asks, "What is cooperation?" (Cooperation is learning how to get along with others, share, take turns, compromise, and resolve conflicts peacefully. Cooperation encourages children to problem-solve to accomplish their goals while getting along with others).

Divide the children into small groups (three or four in each group depending on the age of the children). The larger the group, the more difficult the activity is.

Give each group one large piece of drawing paper and some crayons or markers to share.

Exercise #1:

The teacher tells each group they are to draw one picture of a house. Tell them to include certain things in their pictures. For example, your picture should include a:

- Door
- Four Windows
- Chimney
- Family
- Pet
- Yard
- Flowers
- Rainbow

Tell the children to be creative. Stop and think of other things they can include in their pictures.

Each group shares the same piece of drawing paper and crayons. Give the children about ten or fifteen minutes to complete their drawing. Each person in the group has to participate in drawing the picture.

The children should not ask the teacher any questions during the ten minutes of drawing. Children have to figure out how to cooperate peacefully to complete the drawing.

When the teacher says, "begin" all groups start their drawings at the same time and end when the teacher says, "stop."

After the ten minutes are up let each group talk about what happened during the activity. For example, ask the following questions:

- Did everyone participate in the drawing? Why?
- When the teacher said "begin", did everyone immediately pick up the crayons and begin to draw or did you stop and think of a plan before you began to draw?
- Were their any conflicts within your group? If so, how did you solve them?
- Did everyone share his or her ideas?
- Did everyone draw at the same time or did your group take turns?
- How did you decide who drew what in the picture?
- Did anyone feel upset or frustrated? Why? If yes, how did you handle those feelings?

- Were people treating each other like velvet or sandpaper?
- What do you think you could have done differently to help your group work together without any conflicts?

Encourage children to discuss those questions with each other.

The teacher discusses with the children what it means to "organize your thoughts."

Organizing your thoughts means to:

- Stop and think.
- Make a plan.
- Put your thoughts and ideas in order, what do you need to do first?
- Carry out your thoughts and ideas to accomplish your goals.

Ask the children, "How can organizing your thoughts and ideas help to accomplish your goals or complete a task?"

Repeat this activity giving children different things to draw. Encourage children to use their ideas they discussed and the different ways they learned to cooperate and resolve their conflicts peacefully to complete another drawing.

Give children the opportunity to practice using those ideas to get along with others.

Suggestions for pictures to draw:

- Playground
- Train

- Self-Control
- Circle

Teaching Tip:

Encourage the children to stop and think — make a plan and verbalize that plan before they begin their drawings. After the drawing is completed discuss those same questions.

Exercise #2:

Directions:

Divide the children into small groups and tell each group to create a movement sequence. Tell the children a sequence is doing the movements in the correct order that they create. Each person in the group works together and participates in creating the sequence.

The children should not ask the teacher any questions during the time limit they are creating their movement sequences. When time is up the children perform the movement sequences they created.

Play a piece of music (optional) for the children to coordinate their movements to. If using music, tell the children to focus, concentrate, and listen to the way the music moves. Their movements must match the beat and sound of the music.

Remind the children to cooperate and use velvet and silk words/actions to resolve their conflicts peacefully. After the activity is completed ask the same series of questions (from exercise #1) to stimulate a discussion about working together and getting along with others.

Teaching Tip:

Encourage children to organize their thoughts and ideas to create and act out their movements together. It is important to learn how to organize your thoughts and ideas to accomplish your goals.

The teacher asks the following question:

- How can organizing your thoughts and actions help you to get along with others?

Activity #30: Self-Control

Materials Needed:

- The Tortoise and the Hare by Janet Stevens

Directions:

Read the story <u>The Tortoise and the Hare</u> by Janet Stevens. This story illustrates self-control, encouragement, perseverance, and focus.

Questions to discuss with the children:

- What was the tortoise's goal?
- Did the tortoise have self-control?
- How did the tortoise show that he had his thoughts organized to accomplish his goal?
- How did the tortoise use self-control to win the race?
- Did the hare have self-control? How do you know the hare didn't have self-control?
- What is perseverance? How did perseverance help the tortoise win the race?
- What is focus? How did focus help the tortoise win the race?
- What is encouragement? Why is encouragement important?
- What were the negative consequences for the hare for not using self-control?
- What were the positive consequences for the turtle for using self-control?
- Discuss the importance of mental/emotional strength and how it is used to make positive choices.
- What are the positive consequences for using self-control to calm your thoughts and your body?

What is the Tortoise or the Turtle Principle? (Using self-control, staying focused on what you are doing, and being able to stop and think before you decide what to do).

Discuss with the children how they can use the Tortoise or the Turtle Principle to remind them to stay focused and use self-control.

When children are moving fast and need to slow down, remind them to use the Tortoise or the Turtle Principle to organize their thoughts and take control of their bodies.

Teach the **Tortoise/Turtle** pose.

Turtle/Tortoise

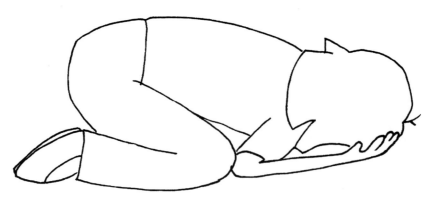

Activity #31: Be Prepared

Materials Needed:

- Music with various rhythms and tempos. I like to use instrumental pieces.

Directions:

Select a piece of quiet, smooth, and slow music for the children to listen to.

Exercise #1:

Ask your students the following questions:

- Can you see the music? (No)
- Can you hear the music? (Yes)

The teacher tells the children to focus on the music. The teacher asks:

What do you focus on when you can't see the music? (You focus on the way the music sounds).

The teacher tells the children to describe the way the music sounds or moves, for example, I hear slow, calm, quiet, smooth, gentle, and peaceful music.
Tell the children to draw a picture of what the music looks like to them or the way the music makes them feel.
Repeat this activity by choosing music with various rhythms and tempos for the children to listen to, describe, and draw pictures of what they visualize (what something looks like in your mind when you can't see it) the music looks like.

Exercise #2:

Directions:

Tell the children to sit in their **Peace** poses and visualize they are going to the beach. The teacher says, "Name some things you need to take with you so you are prepared when you are at the beach."

Examples:

- Bathing Suit
- Goggles
- Sandals

- Sunglasses
- Hat
- Sunblock

The teacher asks:

- Why do you need to take all of those things with you to the beach? (So you are prepared to be outside or go swimming).
- Do you feel confident that you have everything you need to go swimming?
- Where are you going to put all of those things? (In a backpack or suitcase).

The teacher says, "Visualize you are going somewhere that is very cold and snowing. Name some things you need to take with you so you are prepared."

Examples:

- Coat
- Gloves
- Hat
- Boots
- Scarf

The teacher asks:

- Why do you need to take all of those things with you? (So you are prepared to stay warm in the cold weather).
- Do you feel confident that you have everything you need to stay warm in the cold weather?
- Where are you going to put all of those things? (In a backpack or suitcase).

The teacher says, "Visualize all of those things you need to take with you so you are prepared to calm your thoughts and your body."

Examples:

- **Quiet & Still** pose
- **Peace** pose
- STAR (p. 127)
- Glitter Jar (p. 61)
- Velvet Words/Actions (p. 94)
- Deep Breath
- Confidence
- Perseverance
- Mental Strength
- Self-Talk

The teacher asks:

(1) Why do you need to take all of those things with you to calm your thoughts and your body?

- So you are prepared to stop and think and — make responsible (positive) choices.
- So you have everything you need to handle yourself if you're feeling sad, frustrated, angry, or upset.
- To control your thoughts, your body, and your actions.

(2) How are you going to use all of those things? (If I'm upset or angry, I will visualize my STAR and ask myself: *if I choose to do this, what could happen*)?

(3) Where are you going to put all of those things? (Inside your body or your brain).

- Do you feel confident that you have everything you need to calm your thoughts and your body?
- Why is it important to practice all of those things (skills) you need to control your body? (The more I practice, the better I get at controlling my actions. The more confidence I have in myself).
- Why is it important to have with you at all times the things you need to control your actions?

Teaching Tips:

- Discuss with your students how you should always take with you (wherever you go) those things you need to calm your thoughts and your body to make responsible choices.
- This is empowering for children and adults when they realize that they have with them at all times the skills they need to control their actions.
- How do you prepare yourself to become competent using self-control and handling challenging situations? Practice. Children need to be given the opportunity to role-play and discuss how they plan to handle various situations before they occur.
- The key to self-control is practice! Practice encourages competence! Competence encourages confidence!

Exercise #3:

Directions:

Turn on some calm music (optional). Tell your students to sit in the **Quiet & Still, Relax,** or **Peace** pose.

Have your students practice peacefulness and calmness by visualizing all of these things (skills) you have with you at all times to calm your thoughts and your body.

Give children the opportunity to practice these essential skills — stop, think, and control your actions!

Activity #32: Listening

Materials Needed:

- Copy and print the following illustration of the **Tilt** pose.

Directions:

The teacher says to the children, "We learn by listening. Follow the directions by hearing and remembering the words. Focus on the words you hear (do NOT show the **Tilt** pose). Let's learn the **Tilt** pose by listening."

The teacher gives the following directions:

- Stand with your feet together and your hands by your sides. Your back should be straight and your shoulders down.
- Slowly stretch your right arm out to the right side of your body.
- Slowly stretch your left arm out to the left side of your body.
- Lift your left foot near the floor and bend your left knee.
- Slightly bend your right knee.
- Slowly bend and tilt your body to the right side. Your arms stay straight.
- Concentrate and balance for a few seconds. Focus on your body (without looking at it).
- Repeat on the other side.

After reading the directions, show the **Tilt** pose.

The teacher asks the following question:

- Why is it important to listen and remember the words you hear?

Repeat this activity by using yoga positions or the poses and moving balances from the book *Discover ME*.

Give children the opportunity to demonstrate the poses by listening to the directions without seeing the illustrations.

Activity #33: Listening

Materials Needed:

(1) A variety of music with different rhythms and tempos.

(2) Various objects to represent the way the music sounds and moves, such as:

- Cotton.
- Feathers.
- Silk or smooth fabric.
- A picture of a turtle.
- A picture of a rabbit.
- A lightweight (2 lb.).
- A variety of colors (crayons or pictures of colors).
- A drum.
- Pictures to illustrate various emotions, such as happy, sad, angry, excited, etc.
- A small bottle of glitter.
- A ball.

Directions:

Tell the children you are going to play some music. The teacher tells them to listen to the music and focus on the way the music sounds and moves. The children are to describe how the music sounds by matching the way the music moves to the various objects they have to choose from.

For example, if you are listening to a piece of soft, smooth, quiet, and slow music you would match the music to cotton, feathers, silk, and the turtle. All of these objects describe the way the music sounds and moves.

Other suggestions:

- Loud music would be matched to the drum.
- Fast music would be matched to the rabbit.
- Sad music would be matched to the sad face.
- Light music would be matched to a light color.
- Heavy, strong, powerful music would be matched to the drum and the weight.

Next, the teacher puts the objects away and tells the children to listen to the music and visualize the different ways they hear the music move.

Play a variety of music and tell the children to focus on the sound of the music and match their bodies to the way the music moves.

It's not a match if the children are moving their bodies aimlessly and not in time to the music. It's only a match if you are moving to the beat of the music or if the music motivates a certain feeling by its sound, for example, skipping cheerfully to happy music or moving sadly to sad music.

Encourage children to be creative and think of different ways to move to the music. You cannot copy someone else's movement.

This motivates children to use their imaginations and create different movements. Remind the children to listen carefully to the way the music sounds and moves.

Activity #34: Focus, Concentration, & Visualization

Directions:

The teacher says to the children, "What do you focus on when you can't see something? You focus and concentrate on your thoughts and ideas. Your thoughts and ideas are in your mind. When you focus on something you can't see, you visualize it. You think about what it looks like inside your mind."

For example, we can't see a flower right now, but we can visualize (think about) what a flower looks like in our mind and describe it.

Focus means to think about and concentrate on what you are doing.

Exercise #1:

The teacher says create a picture of your bedroom inside your mind and focus on it. Think about and visualize what your room looks like so you can describe it.

Focus on your bedroom:

- What color are the walls?
- Name something that's in your bedroom.
- What kind of pictures do you have in your room or on your walls?
- What else do you keep in your room?
- What color are your sheets? Bedspread?

Other suggestions to focus on, visualize, and describe:

(1) Focus on your pet:

- What kind of pet is it?
- What is his name?
- What color is it?
- What does your pet like to do?

- Is it big or small?
- How do you take care of your pet?
- Where does your pet sleep?
- How do you treat your pet?

(2) Focus on your tricycle or bicycle.

(3) Focus on yourself.

Exercise #2:

Materials Needed:

- Pieces of white drawing paper for each person.
- Crayons
- Various objects or pictures.

Directions:

Choose various objects or pictures for the children to focus on, such as people, places, or things.

Allow the children to focus on each object or picture for about thirty seconds, then take it away.

Next, tell the children to focus on one of those objects or pictures without seeing it. Tell them to visualize or create an image of what that object or picture looked like in their minds.

The teacher says to focus on the image they created in their minds and describe it. Focus on the object and visualize its shape, color, texture, or what it's used for. Describe the object from memory.

After describing those objects or pictures, tell the children to choose one of the objects they focused on and draw a picture of what it looked like.

Continually remind the children to create a picture and visualize what it looked like in their minds. The teacher says to the children, "Focus on the object in your imagination and draw it from memory."

After the children have completed their drawings show them the objects they drew. Tell the children to see if they visualized and included all of the details of their object in their pictures from memory.

Exercise #3:

Materials Needed:

- Pieces of white drawing paper for each person.
- Crayons.
- Where the Sidewalk Ends by Shel Silverstein (or any book of poems or excerpts from a storybook).

Directions:

The teacher reads a poem or an excerpt from a story. Children use visualization skills to illustrate the passages read to them from the story or poem.

Tell the children to focus on the words they hear by using their imaginations to visualize mental images (pictures) of the story.

Tell the children to listen to the words the teacher is reading. When the teacher finishes reading the excerpt from the story, tell the children to draw a picture of the words. Tell them to visualize the story they hear and illustrate it with their drawings.

Teaching Tip:

Visualization encourages abstract thought — planning and organizing your ideas mentally to accomplish your goals. Visualization also encourages reading comprehension.

Exercise #4:

Materials Needed:

- A piece of white drawing paper for each person.
- Crayons.
- Illustration of the **Peace** pose.

Tell the children to sit in the **Peace** pose. Take deep breaths and visualize yourself doing things that are fun — things that make you feel good about yourself. Breathe in your positive thoughts and gently blow away all of the negative thoughts.

Peace

After you have given the children a few minutes to practice their breathing and visualization tell them to draw a picture of themselves doing something that is fun or something that makes them feel good about themselves.

Teaching Tip:

The skill of visualization is used to calm your thoughts and your body by creating mental images of positive thoughts and ideas.

Exercise #5:

Materials Needed:

- Various objects placed on a tray in a specific way. For example: a blue ball inside a red cup, a paper plate on top of a book, a spoon next to a flower in a vase, etc.
- A list of the objects being used (for teachers use only).
- Towel.

Directions:

Discuss visualization with your students. Visualization is creating a picture of what something looks like in your mind without seeing it.

"Let's see what it feels like to stay focused and concentrate on what you are doing and your surroundings."

The teacher tells the children to focus on the tray of objects. After focusing on the tray of objects for about forty-five seconds (depending on the age of the children), the teacher covers the tray with a towel.

Children are asked to name the objects and where the objects were placed on the tray from memory. The teacher tells them to remember by visualizing the tray of objects. Create a mental image of the objects and where they were placed.

You may want to have the older children write the objects down and where they were placed on the tray.

Ask your students:

How can being aware of (or focusing on) yourself, your surroundings, and the actions of others help you to avoid compromising or dangerous situations?

Teaching Tip:

Visualization encourages children to organize their thoughts, strengthen memory skills, and increases self-awareness by creating mental images.

Encourage children to visualize what could happen by the choices they make.

Activity #35: Self-Control

Materials Needed:

- Copy and print the illustrations of the following poses for the children to learn and demonstrate.

Directions:

The teacher explains to the children that it takes self-control, focus, and concentration to balance. Holding poses and positions or moving your bodies while balancing requires mental strength. Encourage the children to hold each pose and maintain their balance for several seconds.

Exercise #1:

The children practice the following poses. Encourage them to focus and concentrate on their bodies to balance. Ask the children, "How do you focus on your body without looking at it?" (By concentrating on what you are doing).

Teaching Tip:

Balancing requires complete mental attention on your body. Balancing activities encourage the connection between the mind and body. This encourages children to use their positive thoughts to take control of their actions by controlling their bodies.

This inspires self-control and focus through body awareness (mentally, emotionally, & physically) — understanding how self-control is used to achieve your goals.

- Through body awareness children begin to understand their bodies, what their bodies are capable of, and that they are responsible for their bodies.
- Through body awareness children begin to understand the importance of being mentally and emotionally in control of yourself (your thoughts and your actions) and that YOU are responsible for the things you choose to say and do.

This activity is designed to encourage self-control by focusing on your positive thoughts to complete your goals while ignoring distractions.

Before the children begin their balances remind them to:

- Stop & think.
- Take a deep breath.
- Organize their thoughts and their bodies.
- Focus on their bodies (without looking at it).
- Ask themselves, *how should I move my body to accomplish this balance?*

Poses and Moving Balances

Tilt

- Concentrate and balance.
- Repeat on the other side.

Reaching

- Balance on your opposite hand and foot.
- Focus on the floor.
- Hold for a few seconds.
- Change and balance on your other hand and foot.

Bridge

Melt

Demonstrate this pose by listening to the following directions read by the teacher.

- Stand on your tiptoes.
- Your arms and your hands should be stretched above your head.
- Gently and slowly lower or melt your body all the way down to the floor without a sound.
- Quietly relax your body in a comfortable position while taking several deep breaths.

Ankle Balance

Ankle Balance: More difficult.

- Focus on your foot.
- Hold for a few seconds. Change and hold on to your other ankle and balance.

Turtle

Peace

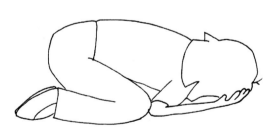

Circle of Peace

Bow & Arrow

- Concentrate and balance.
- Repeat on the other foot.

Twinkling Star

Tree

- Gently and slowly wiggle your fingers and shoulders.
- Concentrate on keeping your lower body still.

Rising Star

Quiet & Still – Sitting

Quiet & Still – Standing

"L"

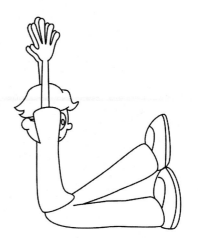

Lift

Sideways

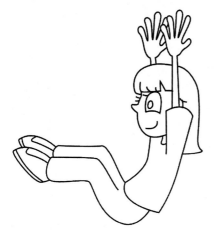

Cooperation Poses

Mountain

Canoeing

- Children coordinate their bodies with each other by leaning forward and backward at the same time.
- Children lean forward with straight arms.
- Children lean back while bending their elbows.
- This should be a quiet, smooth, and continuous movement as if rowing a boat.
- This movement can be done with two or more children.

Bridge

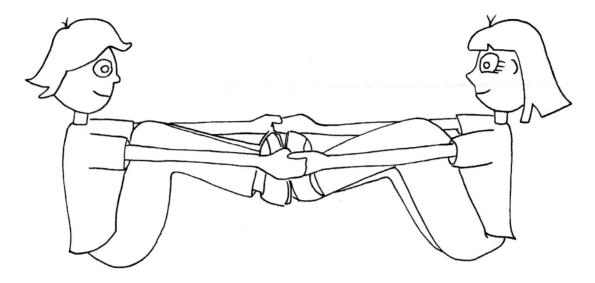

Bicycle Built For Two

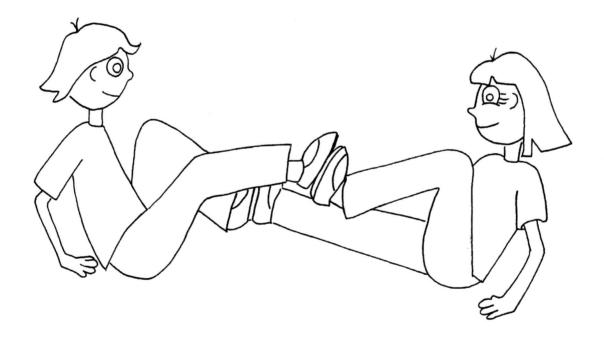

- Children coordinate their bodies with each other by moving their feet back and forth as if pedaling a bicycle.

Exercise #2:

Directions:

To increase the level of difficulty, the teacher creates distractions while the children are balancing in their poses. The teacher encourages them to maintain their self-control, focus, and strengthen their connection between the body and mind. The teacher says, "Encourage your body to listen to your positive thoughts."

For example, while the children are balancing, the teacher blows bubbles all around their bodies or tosses soft sponges or feathers towards them as in activity #5, exercise #3.

Think of other ways to provide distractions, such as have one child try to distract the others who are balancing, by talking to them or jumping up and down in front of them.

Encourage the children to use their mental strength to stay focused, maintain their balance, and ignore the distractions.

For younger children, the poses do not have to be perfect. The goal is to encourage and experience self-control, focus, balance, coordination, and the connection between the body and mind through mental, emotional, and body awareness.

Repeat this activity by balancing in other poses, such as, yoga or the poses and moving balances from the book *Discover ME.*

The teacher asks the following questions:

- How do you feel when you can control your thoughts and your body?
- What were you thinking about to stay focused?
- How can you improve your balancing skills?
- How did you handle the distractions (feathers, bubbles, or other people) to continue balancing? Or how does self-control help you ignore distractions?
- How can you use "visualization" to help you focus?
- How can "self-talk" help you to stay focused and balance?
- How can you use your mind or brain to control your actions in a positive way?

Have the children practice the poses. After continually practicing the poses for a length of time, repeat the above questions.

Also ask:

- Do the poses become easier, the more you practice them?
- Do you feel your balancing, focus, and self-control have improved?
- Do you feel more confident in the skills you need to balance (or control yourself), such as, self-control, focus, or positive thoughts, the more you practice them?
- How can self-control, focus, or positive thoughts help you to take control of your behavior (control your impulses/actions) when someone is teasing you, not letting you play, or have a turn?

Activity #36: Role-Playing

Directions:

Set up role-playing situations with the children. Give them the opportunity to practice the positive skills they have learned to handle the following situations. Have the children role-play and discuss these scenarios. You may need to adapt the questions and situations to fit the needs and ages of your students.

Examples:

What are the positive and negative consequences for your choices? What should you do if:

- Someone pushed you down on the playground?
- Your friends said, "you can play with us, but we don't want the person you're with to play with us?"
- Your friend tries talking you into doing something that you don't feel good about?
- A stranger tried to buy you some ice cream?
- Someone tries to talk you into doing something that you feel could be dangerous to yourself or others?

Ask the children:

- How do you feel about yourself when you know what to do or how to handle a difficult situation?
- Do you feel confident when you are prepared and know what to do?
- How does focusing on your positive thoughts (what you should do) help you to ignore distractions?
- How does visualization and self-talk help you to deal with unkind words? Give an example of visualization.
- How does self-talk help you to remember what you are supposed to do? Give an example of "self-talk."
- Why is it important to tell an adult if someone is treating you or others unkindly?

Activity #37: Focus, Concentration, & Listening

Directions:

The teacher explains to the children that focusing and concentrating means to look at something or someone and to think about what you are doing and looking at.

Exercise #1:

- Have two children stand back to back.
- When you say turn around, the two children turn around and focus on each other. Encourage the children to visualize and create a picture in their minds of the other person's clothes, hair, shoes, eyes, etc.
- Give children about thirty seconds to focus and concentrate on each other.
- When time is up the children turn around and stand back to back again.
- Ask the children to take turns describing each other and what they were wearing.

Set up a role-playing situation by telling the children to pretend they can't find their friend. Have one child describe a friend. Ask the others to guess who is being described.

Exercise #2:

This activity requires partners.

Materials Needed:

If two children are playing this game you will need two sets of identical objects.

For example:

- Two Red Sponges
- Two Blocks
- Two Cups

- Two Blue Sponges
- Two Books
- Two Keys

Each person should have a set of those identical objects.

If there are ten children you will need ten sets of identical objects for each person.

Directions:

There are three ways to play the following focusing and listening game. Children choose a partner. Each partner should have a set of identical objects.

Game #1:

Partners face each other. Choose one person to be the leader.

- The leader has a certain amount of time (1 or 2 minutes, depending on the age of your students) to create a design or pattern with his or her objects.
- When finished the other person creates the identical design (in the same amount of time given) with his or her objects. That person imitates the same pattern, created by the leader, by focusing on his or her design.

Each person takes turns being the leader.

Game #2:

Partners face each other. Choose one person to be the leader.

- The leader has a certain amount of time to create a design or pattern with his or her objects.
- When finished the other person has a certain amount of time to focus on the design, created by the leader, to remember the pattern. When time is up that person turns around so he or she cannot see the leader's design. That person is given a certain amount of time to create the identical pattern with his or her objects from memory.

Each person takes turns being the leader.

Game #3:

Partners sit back to back. Choose one person to be the speaker and the other person to be the listener.

- The speaker is given a certain amount of time to create a design with his or her objects. When finished the speaker gives directions to the listener on how to create the design without the listener seeing it.
- The listener tries to create the identical design with his or her objects by following the directions given by the speaker.

For example, the speaker creates the following design with his or her objects then gives these directions to the listener (his or her partner):

- Put the red sponge on top of the book.
- Put the block on top of the sponge.
- Put the cup on top of the block.
- Put the key inside the cup.

Partners take turns being the speaker and the listener.

Reminders:

- The more objects, the more difficult the activity.
- A timer is recommended to give each person the same amount of time when it is his or her turn.
- The person waiting for his or her turn waits patiently (in **Peace** pose).

When finished, the teacher discusses the importance of focusing, listening, concentrating, and being patient.

Activity #38: Self-Control & Consequences

Directions:

The teacher explains to the children that self-control is being able to stop your body and think about the positive and negative consequences of your choices (your actions). Consequences are when you ask yourself, *if I choose to do this, what could happen?* Or when something happens what comes next?

Sometimes we have no control over the things that happen, but we do have control over the things we say and do. We can control how we choose to handle various situations. Our choices can influence the outcome of a situation.

Teaching Tip:

It's important that children and adults understand that they can control their actions and that there are positive and negative consequences for the things they choose to say and do.

Discuss with your students the following questions to encourage an understanding of consequences. You may want to adapt the questions to fit the needs of your class.

What could happen and what are the consequences if:

- There were no telephones?
- It never rained?
- There was a tornado? Can you control the weather? Even though you can't control the weather, what choices can you make to be prepared for bad weather?
- It was snowing outside and you wore shorts and sandals to school?
- You didn't study for a test?
- You took something that didn't belong to you?
- Someone pushed you down?
- Someone called you a name that wasn't nice?
- You left your toys on the stairs?
- You never brushed your teeth?
- You didn't have any friends?
- You did not focus or concentrate on what you were doing?
- You did focus or concentrate on what you were doing?

- You used self-control before you made a decision?
- You did not use self-control before you made a decision?
- You apologized to someone for doing something wrong?
- You did not apologize for doing something wrong?
- You paid attention to what you were doing?
- You did not pay attention to what you were doing?
- You always ate sweets and candy?
- Your friend forgot their lunch and you gave them half of your lunch?
- You pushed someone down?
- You helped your friend learn to ride a bike?
- You cleaned your room?
- No one used self-control?

Discuss with your students what the positive consequences are for doing the following things listed below and what the negative consequences are for not doing them?

- Cleaning your room.
- Sharing your toys.
- Listening to the directions.
- Going to bed early and getting plenty of sleep.
- Telling an adult if someone is treating you or others unkindly.
- Standing up for your friends.

The teacher asks:

- Why is it important to tell a teacher or parent that you are feeling angry or upset and that you don't know how to deal with this feeling?
- Why is it important to stop and think about the consequences for what you choose to say and do?

Activity #39: Focus & Concentration

Materials Needed:

- Various objects of different sizes, weights, shapes, textures, and colors.
- A list of all the objects being used (for teacher's use only).
- Towel.

Directions:

Tell the children to sit in a circle in a person-space pattern (a space between their bodies so their bodies are not touching).

In the middle of the circle place the various objects of different sizes, weights, shapes, textures, and colors. The more objects used, the more difficult the activity.

The teacher covers the objects with a towel. The teacher says to the children, "I am going to call out an object, such as, a bear (the teacher refers to the list of objects he or she is using). When I remove the towel, quickly find the bear with your eyes and — focus and concentrate on it." Remind the children to focus on the details of the bear.

When time is up the teacher covers the objects. Encourage the children to visualize what the bear looked like in their minds. The teacher asks questions about the bear such as,

- What color was the bear?
- What color were his eyes?
- What was the bear wearing?

Ask detailed questions about the objects to encourage self-control, focus, and concentration.

After the activity is completed, the teacher asks the following questions:

- Why is it important to focus on your feelings or to be aware of your feelings?
- Why is it important to be aware of other people's feelings?
- Why is it important to focus and concentrate on your thoughts and actions?

Activity #40: Focus

Materials Needed:

- Soccer or basketball.

Directions:

- The teacher bounces the ball. Tell the children to focus on the ball and watch it as it bounces.

Exercise #1:

- The teacher tells the children to focus on the ball and clap their hands each time the ball bounces. Their hands should clap each time the ball touches the floor. The teacher bounces the ball in various ways such as close to the floor (short bounces) or far away from the floor (long bounces).
- Next, tell the children to focus on the ball and jump each time the ball bounces.
- When jumping children try to touch their feet to the floor at the same time the ball touches the floor. Children focus on the ball while trying to coordinate their jumping with the bouncing of the ball.
- Remind the children to stop, think, and take a deep breath before they begin.
- Tell the children to focus on the ball and concentrate on coordinating their brains (thoughts) and their bodies (actions). Coordinating your brain and your body means your body is doing what your brain (thoughts) tells it to do. Your brain (thoughts) and your body (actions) are working together. Organize your thoughts and your body (actions).

Next, give one child the ball to bounce. The teacher tells the child to:

- Stop, think, and take a deep breath before he or she begins.
- Focus on the ball and begin bouncing it.
- Jump each time the ball touches the floor. Concentrate on trying to touch your feet to the floor at the same time the ball touches the floor.

Exercise #2:

Materials Needed:

- Soccer ball or any type of medium-sized ball that you can write on.
- Erasable Marker.
- Paper and pencil for each child.

Directions:

The teacher uses an erasable marker to write various words or numbers on the ball or you can mark the ball with a specific color or colors (for younger children).

Tell the children to form a circle in a person – space pattern (a space between each person so their bodies are not touching) and sit in their **Peace** poses.

Give each child a piece of paper and a pencil.

- Tell the children to focus on the ball while the teacher is bouncing it. Children work at maintaining their focus and try to figure out what words or numbers are written on the ball while the teacher is bouncing it.
- The teacher bounces the ball for a few seconds. When time is up, the teacher puts the ball away so no one can see it.
- The teacher calls on one child to name what numbers were written on the ball or ask the children to write down what numbers were written on the ball.
- Continue this game by erasing the numbers or words on the ball and writing different ones on it each time.

Teaching Tip:

Instead of yelling out the numbers they see on the ball, children have to control their impulses. Encourage children to stop and think by writing the numbers down or wait for their name to be called before they can answer.

The teacher asks the children:

- What does it mean to coordinate your thoughts and actions?

After the activity is finished have the children sit in their **Quiet and Still** poses. The teacher says, "Organize your thoughts and your bodies (actions). Coordinate your brain (thoughts) and your bodies (actions). Use your thoughts to tell your body to take deep breaths, relax, and calm down."

Self-control and focus are using your positive thoughts to control your body.

The teacher discusses the following questions with the children,

- Why is it important for your body to listen to your positive thoughts?
- Why is it important to organize your thoughts and ideas before you do something?
- How do you feel when you know you are strong enough to take charge (control) of your own body (your actions)?
- Does it help you feel prepared (confident) when you know how to handle difficult situations in a positive way? Why?

Exercise #3:

Directions:

Set up role-playing and/or discussions to give children the opportunity to practice using positive ways to deal with various situations. If necessary, adapt the situations to fit the needs of your class.

Each time a scenario is read to the class the teacher asks:

(1)   Are these words and actions velvet or sandpaper?
(2)   Just imagine! How would you feel if this happened to you?
(3)   How would you respond or handle this situation?

Remind students to take a deep breath and stop and think before they answer.

Scenarios:

- Someone calls you a name that hurts your feelings.
- You ask your friends if you can play with them and they all shout, NO!
- When standing in line your friend is always pushing and shoving trying to make you move faster.
- "If you won't do what I want to do, I'm not going to play and you can't be my friend."
- You missed a day at school because you were sick and your friend called to see if you were ok.
- Someone said to you, "You can't play with us because you talk funny." The friend you were with said, "She's my friend and if she can't play we'll both leave and do something else."
- "Ha ha ha, you look so funny in those pants! They are so ugly!"
- "If you take his lunch money out of his backpack, we'll let you play with us."
- "Thank-you for asking me to eat lunch with you." "I just started school here and I don't know anyone."
- "I don't like to clean up when we finish playing!" "I'm going home now."
- Your friend snatches the book right out of your hands that you are reading and says, "That's the book I want to look at!"
- What happened? Why are you crying? What can I do to help?

Activity #41: Organizing Your Thoughts & Actions

Materials Needed:

- Five or six pieces of elastic. Each piece should be about eight feet long.

Exercise #1:

Directions:

Tie one end of the piece of elastic to the leg of a table and the other end to the leg of another table (tables should be heavy enough so they do not move). Tables should also be placed far enough apart for the elastic to be stretched so it is not touching the floor. The elastic should be at least a foot off the floor.

Give children the opportunity to experiment with the elastic, for example, by crawling under it, jumping over it, stretching it up with their hands, or stepping on it with their feet to hold it down.

Next, tie five or six pieces of elastic to the legs of the tables to create a maze for the children to experiment with and move through.

The teacher tells the children to stop and think. Plan how you are going to move through the elastic before you begin.

The teacher asks, "How do you plan to move your body through the maze?" Encourage the children to come up with their own ideas.

For example, I'm going to:

- Step over it.
- Crawl under it.
- Jump over it.

- Stretch it over my head.
- Jump over it then crawl under it.

Remember, the children have to verbalize their plans before they begin moving their bodies through the maze.

Teaching Tip:

This gives children the opportunity to stop and think before they act. Children make a plan, verbalize that plan, then act it out.

This gives them the opportunity to coordinate their thoughts and actions. It encourages the connection between the body and mind.

Exercise #2:

Directions:

Children plan how they are going to move their bodies. They verbalize that plan BEFORE they begin moving.

For example, the teacher tells them to think of different ways you can:

- Move your body across the room. (I plan to skip 3 times, turn around once, and jog).
- Move your hands. (I am going to clap my hands twice, rub them together, and put them behind my back).
- Skip. (I am going to skip 4 times loudly, 4 times softly, skip in a circle, then skip backward).
- Move with a partner. (We are going to jog, jump once, and hop on one foot).
- Cooperate in the classroom or on the playground. (We plan to take turns and share).
- Use self-control in the classroom, on the playground, or at home. (I am going to stop & think before I decide what to do).

The teacher discusses the following questions with the children.

- How do you plan to cooperate before you begin playing a game?
- How do you plan to use self-control before I begin reading a story?
- How do you plan to calm your thoughts and your body when you are feeling angry, upset, or frustrated? Or how do you plan to control your actions when you are feeling angry, upset, or frustrated?
- How do you plan to use self-control at the dinner table?
- How can organizing your thoughts and ideas help you to accomplish your goals? Or why is it important to organize your thoughts and ideas?

Activity #42: Focus, Concentration, & Memory

Materials Needed:

- Various objects, such as, a ball, block, key, doll, and glove.
- Different things to hide the objects in or under, such as a box, cup, bag, or underneath a bowl. If you have ten objects you will need ten different things to hide each one in or underneath.
- A list of all the objects being used (for teacher's use only).

Directions:

Have the children sit in a circle in a person-space pattern (a space between their bodies so their bodies are not touching).

The teacher explains that focus means to look at something or someone and to think about what you are doing and looking at.

Exercise #1:

Tell the children to focus on the various objects while the teacher is hiding them. The children watch the teacher as he or she hides each object.

For example, the ball is hidden underneath the bowl, the key is hidden in the cup, the block is hidden inside a box, and so on. You should not be able to see any part of the hidden object.

The teacher tells the children to focus and remember where each object is hidden. The more objects you hide increase the difficulty of the activity.

Tell the children to stop and think. The teacher calls out the name of one child and asks, "Where is the ball hidden?" Continue this format asking one child at a time where each object is hidden.

Instead of yelling out where each object is hidden children have to control their impulses. Encourage children to wait for their names to be called before they answer.

For older children, you may want them to write down where each object is hidden.

Exercise #2:

Directions:

Children sit in a circle in a person-space pattern. The teacher hides each object underneath a box, cup, inside a bag, etc. The teacher tells the children to watch and remember where each object is hidden.

After hiding the objects tell the children to jog (in the same direction) for about thirty seconds. When the teacher says, "stop" the children return to the circle and sit in their same space in a person-space pattern. The teacher calls out the name of one child and asks: "Where is the block hidden?"

Continue this format. Give children the opportunity to jog, skip, or gallop and then return to the circle sitting in their same space in a person-space pattern. The teacher asks, "Where is the glove hidden?"

Teaching Tip:

Ask the children to name some different things they can do to help them remember.

For example,

- Focus
- Self-Talk (repeat the directions to yourself).
- Look at the person who is talking.

- Concentrate.
- Stop & Think.

Activity #43: Self-Control, Focus, & Concentration

Materials Needed:

- Copy and print the illustrations of the following poses for the children to learn and demonstrate.

Directions:

Show the children the illustration of the **Kitty Cat Stretch** and **Table-Top Tummy.** The teacher explains to the children that it takes self-control and focus to make your body move in different ways.

Give children the opportunity to practice the poses. The teacher tells them to control their bodies, focus, and concentrate on moving smoothly, gently, and quietly. Hold each pose for several seconds.

Kitty Cat Stretch

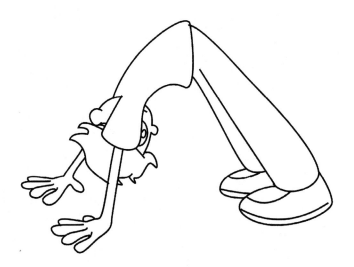

Table -Top Tummy

After the children have practiced the poses the teacher says:

- Begin by balancing in the **Kitty Cat Stretch**. Focus on your feet. Hold this pose (for a few seconds) and balance. Tell the children to slowly count to five while holding each pose. Keep your body still.
- From this position slowly move your body into the **Table-Top Tummy** pose. Balance (for a few seconds). Slowly count to five.
- Move your body from **Table-Top Tummy** back to **Kitty Cat Stretch.**
- Moving your body from one position to another should be a smooth, quiet, and continuous movement.
- Control your body and move from the **Kitty Cat Stretch** to **Table-Top Tummy** and back into the **Kitty Cat Stretch** three times.

Tell the children when moving from the **Kitty Cat Stretch** to **Table-Top Tummy** (and vice versa) only your hands and feet should be touching the floor. Before beginning this movement sequence remind the children to:

- Stop & think.
- Take a deep breath.
- Focus on the movement of your body.
- Ask yourself, *how should I move my body?*
- Hold each pose while you slowly count to five.

The teacher asks the following questions:

- What do you focus on when you are balancing in the **Kitty Cat Stretch?**
- Which direction is your tummy facing when you are balancing in the **Kitty Cat Stretch?**
- Where do you focus when you are balancing in the **Table-Top Tummy** pose?
- Which direction is your tummy facing when you are balancing in the **Table-Top Tummy** pose?

Teaching Tip:

This exercise inspires body awareness by encouraging children to focus on the movement of their bodies.

Activity #44: Stop & Think: Organize Your Thoughts!

Directions;

The teacher says to the children, "Control your body, focus, and concentrate. Stop and think before you decide what to do. Remember to focus and organize your thoughts and ideas inside your imagination."

The teacher tells the children to create their own poses or movements (no voices) for the following ideas:

- A flickering candle.
- A tiny seed growing into a flower.
- Honey flowing from a jar.
- Balancing on one body part, two, three, or four.
- A snowman melting in the sunshine.
- Windshield wipers.
- Thunder and lightning.
- The wind.
- Bending.
- A bridge.
- Quickly and quietly.
- Straight.
- Round.

- Paying attention while listening to a story.
- Focusing and concentrating.
- Self-control.
- Crooked.
- Giving.
- Create your own pose and name it.
- A butterfly lost in the clouds.
- A leaf blowing in the wind.
- Walking outside in the winter. Name some words that describe winter.
- Walking on glue.
- Caring for a puppy.
- Walking through a thunderstorm.
- Balancing while moving.

The teacher reminds the children to pay attention to their bodies and create a movement (no voices) for:

- Powerful.
- Gentle.
- Tall.
- Short.
- Slow.
- Fast.
- Sad.
- Angry.
- Joyful.

- Smooth.
- Bumpy.
- 3-part movement, such as, jump, clap, & step.
- Include 2 claps in a quiet movement.
- Happiness.
- Confidence.
- Calm & Peaceful.

Teaching Tip:

Discuss with the children the various ways they had to move and control their bodies to create a movement or feeling to illustrate those ideas.

This activity inspires body awareness by encouraging children to focus on the movement of their bodies.

Activity #45: Organizing Your Thoughts

Materials Needed:

- Copy and print the illustrations of the following poses.

Directions:

The teacher discusses with the children what it means to organize your thoughts and ideas.

Organizing your thoughts means to:

- Stop and think.
- Put your thoughts in order so your body knows what to do.
- Visualizing your body following the directions of your thoughts.
- Encouraging your body to respond to your thoughts to complete a task or accomplish your goals.

Exercise #1:

The teacher asks the children, "What does the word silence mean? Silence means quiet or no sound. Let's practice being silent."

The teacher tells the children to sit in their **Quiet and Still** poses in silence: no voices, sounds, or movements. Use your self-control to keep your body quiet and still.

Breathe and think about the movement of your breath, the way your body feels, and what it feels like to be silent.

Quiet & Still - sitting

After the children have sat in silence for about 30 seconds (may use a timer) the teacher asks, "What does silence sound and feel like?" When you are silent you can hear your thoughts and hear yourself think. It gives you time to put your thoughts in order.

The teacher tells the children to stand in their **Quiet and Still** poses in silence. (Hold this pose for several seconds).

Quiet & Still - standing

Next, the teacher calls out the following directions for the children to move their bodies in specific ways (no voices). Select a piece of instrumental music for the children to move to (optional).

The teacher reminds the children to use their self-control and focus on the words they hear. Organize your thoughts so your body knows what to do.

The teacher calls out various ways for the children to move their bodies (no voices):

- Walk on your tiptoes. Walk on your heels.
- Gallop.
- Jog (slow running).
- Skip in place. Skip forward. Skip backward.
- Move with good posture.
- Move with your arms above your head while walking, galloping, and skipping.
- Walk with one hand near your foot and the other hand far away from your head.
- Sway.
- Walk with one hand above your waist and the other hand below your head.
- Stand still with one body part swinging gently.
- Walk while circling your hands.
- Walk while wiggling your fingers.
- Sit on the floor without making a sound.
- Crawl forward slowly. Crawl backward slowly.
- Gently roll your body over two times.
- Sit in your **Peace** poses. Take deep breaths. Focus on the way your body feels when you are calm and relaxed.

Peace

Exercise #2:

Directions:

Have the children sit in their **Peace** poses. Tell the children you are going to ask them some questions. Adapt the questions to fit the needs of your students.

Tell the children before they raise their hands to stop and think what the answer is to the question. Wait for your name to be called before you answer.

Take a deep breath and organize your thoughts.

- Name a number between two and five.
- Name a number larger than ten.
- Name a fruit.
- Name a vegetable.
- What number comes after fourteen?
- What color is an apple?
- If you had a horse what would you name it?
- If someone asked you to call your friend a name that wasn't nice what would you do?
- Organize these numbers by putting them in the correct order: smallest to largest. 9, 6, 8, 4, 1.
- Organize your thoughts. What would you do if someone said we don't like you? We don't want you to play with us.
- What would you do if you were at your friend's house and they wanted to play basketball, but you wanted to watch television?
- What would you do if everyone were teasing your friend?
- What number is larger, twelve or nine?
- What should you do if a stranger asks, "Would you like some candy?"
- Why should you not take things from strangers?
- Why is it important to stop and think before you say or do something?

Teaching Tip:

Tell the children they can answer lots of questions and think of great ideas when they remember to stop and think.

The teacher says to the children, "Let's take a body break. Sit in your **Quiet & Still** poses in silence. Breathe in the silence and gently let go (or blow away) of the noise. Focus on your positive thoughts and how your body listens to what your thoughts tell your body to do."

Quiet & Still

The teacher asks, "Why is it important to stop and think before you say or do something?" It's important to control your body and — stay calm and listen to your positive thoughts.

Activity #46: Motor Planning & Sequencing

Directions:

This motor planning and sequencing activity encourages mind-body coordination. It requires self-control, focus, and concentration.

The teacher tells the children, "Let's practice controlling our bodies, our thoughts, and our actions to learn this movement sequence. A sequence is when we do something in order." For example, count to five in sequence: one, two, three, four, five. Count to five out of sequence: two, five, three, one, four.

"This movement sequence has eight parts. Let's all count to eight together (in sequence)."

- Every time you say the number one: Clap your hands one time.
- Every time you say the number two: Tap your legs one time.
- Every time you say the number three: Jump one time.
- Every time you say the number four: Kick one time.
- Every time you say the number five: Stamp your right foot.
- Every time you say the number six: Stamp your left foot.
- Every time you say the number seven: Tap your right hip one time.
- Every time you say the number eight: Tap your left hip one time.

Give children the opportunity to repeat this sequence. The more they practice, the easier this sequence becomes.

Select a piece of music (optional) for the children to perform this sequence to.

The teacher asks the children:

- How does self-control and focus help you to learn this sequence?
- How does self-control and focus help you to make positive choices?

Using this same format make up other movements to coordinate with the numbers one through eight. Give children the opportunity to create their own movements.

For younger children, shorten the sequence and create simpler movements to coordinate with the numbers one through four.

This activity can be as simple or as hard as you need it to be depending on the ages of the children and the movements you create.

Teaching Tip:

Remember to plan activities that are challenging, but with continued practice can be accomplished and provide successful experiences.

It's important that children understand that it takes practice to learn new skills and that it's ok to make a mistake. We don't always learn something the first time we try.

Activity #47: Cooperation

Directions:

The teacher discusses cooperation with the children. Cooperation is a skill. It is learning how to get along with others, share, take turns, compromise, and resolve conflicts peacefully. It encourages children to problem-solve to accomplish their goals while getting along and working with others.

This activity requires a large group to create various body formations. The teacher tells the children to create the following formations or designs with their bodies.

Give the children a certain amount of time to create each formation. Everyone in the group has to participate.

Exercise #1:

The teacher says to the group:

- Form a straight line.
- Form yourselves into a circle. Stand in a person-space pattern — a small space between your bodies so your bodies are not touching.
- Line up in a straight line with a partner.
- Form two straight lines parallel to each other.
- Form a circle with one girl and one boy standing in the middle.
- Form your bodies into various letters, such as H, V, E, C, I, etc.
- Arrange your bodies as if you were sitting in a movie theatre.
- Arrange your bodies from shortest to tallest.
- Arrange your bodies as if you were sitting on an airplane.

The teacher asks the following questions:

- Did you find it difficult to work together in a large group? Why?
- What kind of conflicts did you have? How did you solve them?
- Did everyone participate? Why?
- Did everyone share his or her ideas? Why?
- Did you have to make any compromises in the group? Why?
- Did anyone feel upset or frustrated trying to work with the others? Why? How did you handle those feelings?
- Were people treating each other like velvet or sandpaper? Why?
- What do you think could have been done differently to help your group work together without any conflicts?
- What does it mean to organize your thoughts?
- How can organizing your thoughts help to accomplish your goals or complete a task?

Encourage the children to discuss these questions with each other.

Exercise #2:

Directions:

Repeat exercise #1 dividing the children into smaller groups. Give children the opportunity to create their own ideas to form different body formations.

For example, the teacher may tell each group to choose a number, letter, shape, or object to create with their bodies, such as, one group may choose to form a tree.

Remind the children to use their ideas and the different ways they learned to cooperate with each other to complete their body formations.

When finished performing their creations in smaller groups, the teacher asks the same questions from exercise #1.

The teacher also asks:

Did you find it easier to work together in a smaller or a larger group? Why?

Teaching Tip:

The more opportunities children are given to practice those skills learned to cooperate and resolve conflicts peacefully, the more confident they become in themselves.

This encourages children to use those same skills in other challenging situations with self-control and confidence.

Activity #48: Mind-Body Connection

Materials Needed:

- A selection of music with various rhythms.
- Masking Tape.
- A large open space so the children have room to move.

Directions:

The teacher places pieces of masking tape in a random pattern on the floor. For example, if you have ten children you will need ten pieces of tape. Each person stands on a piece of tape and is given a number (one through ten) to remember.

Exercise #1:

The teacher calls out the numbers (one through ten) several times to give the children the opportunity to practice remembering their numbers. For example, tell the children to raise their hands or stand up every time their number is called. Begin with number one and call out the numbers in sequence and then call the numbers out-of-sequence.

Next, tell the children to sit on their piece of tape in their **Peace** poses and listen to the music. The teacher tells the children to focus on the sound of the music and the way the music moves. Give children some time to focus on the music and discuss with them the way the music moves, for example, do you hear smooth, fast, slow, bumpy, quiet, gentle, calm, or peaceful music?

After giving the children the opportunity to listen to the music, tell them to match their bodies to the sound of the music while sitting on their tape. It has to be a specific movement that matches the way the music moves.

Next, the children stand on their piece of tape and illustrate the way the music moves with their bodies.

Tell the children to think of how they can create a movement sequence or pattern to match the music. Use your own ideas to create a movement pattern that is different from everyone else's.

Give the children some time to experiment with moving their bodies around the room to the music. After several minutes, children return to their tape and sit in their **Peace** poses. Always give the children several seconds to calm their bodies and breathe while sitting in their poses.

Next, the teacher calls out their numbers beginning with number one. When their number is called that person stands and performs his or her movement sequence individually.

After all the numbers have been called several times begin calling their numbers out-of-sequence. Each time they hear their number, that person stands and performs their movement. Tell the children to create a different movement to the music each time their number is called.

Teaching Tip:

Choose music with various rhythms to give children the opportunity to describe the music verbally and to create different movement patterns with their bodies. Tell the children to use self-control and focus to control their bodies.

Encourage children to organize their thoughts and ideas with their bodies to create and perform their movement patterns.

Exercise #2:

Directions:

Divide the children into small groups. Each group choreographs their own movement pattern or sequence to the music.

After each group has been given the opportunity to perform their movement sequence, the teacher discusses the following questions:

- Why is it important to listen?
- Why is it important to listen to yourself?
- Why is it important to listen to others?
- What do you focus on when you are listening to the music?
- Why is it important to organize your thoughts and ideas in your brain?
- What is choreography?
- Did everyone participate in creating the movement sequence? Why?
- Did everyone take turns sharing ideas? Why?
- Did the others listen to the ideas that were being shared in the group?
- Did you find it difficult to work together in a group? Why?
- Did anyone feel frustrated or upset trying to work with the others? Why?
- Do you feel you showed respect to the others working in your group?
- Were people acting like velvet or sandpaper? Why?
- What do you think could have been done differently to help your group work together without any conflicts?

Teaching Tip:

When children are participating in an activity that involves taking turns, remind them to wait patiently for their turn by asking themselves, *what should I be doing when it's not my turn?* I should be waiting patiently by respecting the person who is taking their turn. Respect is being kind and thoughtful to others.

The teacher asks the children to name some different ways that you can show respect to others while waiting for your turn, for example:

- Sitting in my **Quiet & Still** or my **Peace** pose.
- Sitting quietly.

- Keeping my body still.
- Using self-control.
- Not interrupting.

Activity #49: Focus, Concentration, & Memory

Materials Needed:

- Pictures of various objects, such as a ball, key, dog, etc. For example, if you have ten children you will need ten different pictures.
- Write down a list of all the pictures you are using (for teacher's use only).

Directions:

Have the children sit in a circle in a person-space pattern (a space between each person so their bodies are not touching).

Tell the children to sit in their **Peace** poses and focus on the teacher.

Exercise #1:

- The teacher says, "I'm going to place a picture card face down in front of your body. When I say "go" pick up your card so no one else can see it. Focus on your picture, remember what it is, and place it face down in front of your body."
- When the teacher says, "begin" all the children hold up their pictures for everyone else to see them.
- Tell everyone to focus on the pictures and remember who has which picture. Allow the children to focus and concentrate on all the pictures for a few seconds or whatever time limit is appropriate depending on the age of the children.
- When the teacher says, "stop" everyone places their pictures face down in front of his or her body.

The teacher refers to the list of pictures and asks the children, "Who had the picture of the ball? The block? The key?" Ask other questions about the pictures, such as color or shape?

Remind the children to control their voices (impulses) by waiting for the teacher to call their names before they answer.

When the game is finished, ask the children, "How did you remember who had which picture?" (By focusing, concentrating, paying attention, or using self-control).

Teaching Tip:

Remind the children it takes self-control to focus, concentrate, and pay attention.

Exercise #2:

Materials Needed:

- Index cards

Directions:

If you have ten children you will need ten index cards. Divide these ten cards into two groups of five. Each group of cards should be numbered from one to five. Each card should have one number written on it. Mix up all the cards together so they are not in the correct order.

Tell the children to sit in their **Peace** poses and focus on the teacher. Say to the children,

- I'm going to place a card face down in front of your body. When I say "go" pick up your cards so no one else can see them. Focus on your number, remember what your number is, then place it face down in front of your body.
- When I say "begin" show your numbers by holding up your cards for everyone else to see them. Allow a few seconds for everyone to focus on all the numbers.
- The teacher tells the children they are looking for the person who has the same number as them.
- When I say "stop" everyone puts their numbers face down in front of his or her body.

The teacher asks the children, "Who has the same number as you?" Remind them to stop, think, and wait for their name to be called.

This activity can also be done by having the children match various pictures of objects, shapes, or letters. Remember you will need two sets of matching pictures.

Pictures that demonstrate opposites can also be used. For example, if you have a picture of a sad face, look for the person who has a happy face.

Activity #50: The Buddy System

The teacher discusses the following questions:

(1) What is the buddy system? The buddy system is when two people are partners. These partners watch out for each other's safety. Each person's responsibility is to know where their partner is, and what to do if they cannot find their partner.

(2) Why is it important to use the buddy system? The buddy system increases your safety and the safety of your partner. It's always safer when you go some place with a buddy. It's important that someone knows where you are at all times. When you go places alone you have a greater chance of being harmed.

(3) What is your responsibility when using the buddy system? To always know where the other person is and that they are safe, to increase your safety and the safety of your partner (buddy), and to know what to do if you feel you or your partner are in danger.

Name a person who could be your buddy:

- Parent
- Sibling
- Baby Sitter

- Teacher
- Friend

Name some places it's important to use the buddy system:

- Park
- Mall
- Movies
- Bike Ride

- Walking to and From School
- Beach/Swimming
- Amusement Park
- Field Trip

Why is it important to use the buddy system? How would you handle the following situations? Also, discuss the consequences of your choices. (You may need to adapt the situations to fit the needs of your students).

(1) You are at the mall and your friend has to go to the bathroom.
(2) You are meeting someone at the movies and you decide to go a different way instead of taking your usual route.
(3) You leave a party early and walk home alone.
(4) You are at the amusement park and leave the group to get something to eat.

<u>Materials Needed:</u>

Music that's easy to walk, gallop, or skip to.

<u>Directions:</u>

Each student writes his or her name on an index card. The teacher mixes up all the cards. Students choose a partner by picking a name.

Students are instructed to move to the music around the room in various ways, such as, walking, galloping, skipping, dancing, etc. Everyone should move in the same direction.

- When the music is playing students move around the room WITHOUT their partners.
- When the music stops the teacher calls out *"buddy check!"* Students quickly find their partners and sit down with each other.

"Buddy check" means its time to stop and check on your buddy and make sure everyone is there.

Continue this format giving the children the opportunity to practice moving around the room WITHOUT their buddies, but when the music stops, they quickly find their partner for a *"buddy check."*

Each time the music stops and the children are sitting with their buddies the teacher asks a question such as,

- What is the buddy system?
- What is your responsibility to your buddy?
- Why is it important to use the buddy system?
- What would you do if you were at the mall and the restrooms were in an isolated area? Would you let your buddy go alone or would you walk with him or her?
- What would you do if you were at the amusement park and your buddy said *I am not feeling well, I'm going to walk home.* What would you do?
- Every time your friend goes to the cafeteria for lunch this bully always bumps into her intentionally and calls her a name. How could it help if you started going to the cafeteria with your friend? If that happened to you how would you feel if your friend said, *I'll walk with you to the cafeteria so you don't have to go alone?*
- Why is it safer to always go some place with another person?
- How does it feel when you know you have someone looking out for your safety?
- If you felt you were in danger and you were all alone, how would you feel and what would you do? How would it help if you were with your buddy?
- Why is it safer to always go some place with another person?

The teacher asks:

- What is responsibility?
- How can self-control (visualize your STAR and what it represents) help you to make a positive choice in the above situations?

Activity #51: When My Eyes Are Closed, I Can Still See Me

Materials Needed:

- Copy and print the illustrations of the following poses for the children to learn and demonstrate.

Directions:

Tell the children to get into the **Relax** pose and close their eyes as the teacher reads the following story, *When My Eyes Are Closed, I Can Still See Me.*

Tell them to focus (pay attention/concentrate) on the words they hear. The teacher says, "Visualize yourself in the story."

Relax

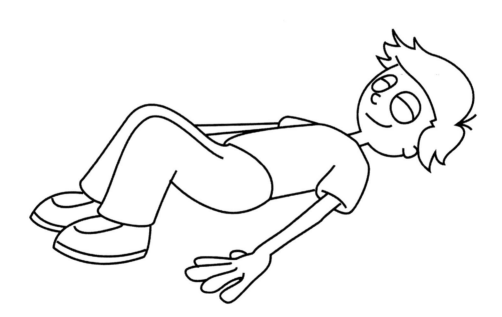

When My Eyes Are Closed, I Can Still See Me

When my eyes are closed, I can still see me — so I take a deep breath and begin to rest with my thoughts and my imagination — on a magnificent quest.

(Pause for a deep breath)

When my eyes are closed, I can still see me.
I see me diving into the glistening sea.

Against the waves, it's hard to push on, but the sea horse cheers, *"Don't give up! You must push along!"*
So over and over I repeat to myself: my arms, my legs, my endurance feel strong — I must persevere, for this journey is long!

When my eyes are closed, I can still see me — so I take a deep breath and continue to rest with my thoughts and my imagination so clearly picturesque.

(Pause for a deep breath)

I can see me swimming in the ocean so free.
I can feel the sun — its warm gentle rays reaching out to me.
I see vibrant colors begin to unfold: yellow, orange, and mystic gold.

I can hear the quiet sounds all around.
The wings of the seagulls flutter up and down.
I hear dolphins whispering as they gently sigh.
I can see them diving like rainbows across the sky.
When my eyes are closed, I can still see me — riding a blue and gray dolphin in and out of the waves.
I see colorful starfish across the ocean sway like emeralds, amethysts, and bright rubies at play.

When my eyes are closed, I can still see me.
I take a deep breath and continue to rest — with my thoughts and my imagination so clearly picturesque.

(Pause for a deep breath)

There's a beautiful rainbow that lights up the sky — from east to west — what a magnificent quest!
The arch is so steep I could see this from afar. Its colorful reflection appears in the stars.

I take a deep breath as I look towards the sky.

(Pause for a deep breath)

How will I know if I don't even try?

Over and over I repeat to myself — I must persevere and overcome the fear. This dream of mine is perfectly clear!

Along the rainbow I reluctantly climb to reach for the sun, the moon, and the stars!
The eagles and the doves begin to cheer, *"Don't give up! You must push along!"*
Over and over I quietly chant: my body, my spirit, my endurance feel strong. I must persevere, for this journey is long.

I take a deep breath and continue my quest.

(Pause for a deep breath)

To the top of the arch I carefully climb, a magnificent feat — my journey's complete.
That golden star is mine to keep!

I take a deep breath and continue to rest — inside my imagination I continue my quest.

(Pause for a deep breath)

So high in the sky I can see myself fly — with strength and determination like an eagle in flight.
I see myself soar above the challenging heights.

I take a deep breath and continue my flight.

(Pause for a deep breath)

I open my eyes.

I take a deep breath.

(Pause for a deep breath)

Over and over I quietly chant — persevere, persevere, I MUST persevere.

When my eyes are closed, I can still see me.
The journey, the dream — it's all very clear!

(Pause for a deep breath)

The teacher shows the illustrations for the **Dolphin** pose for the children to learn and demonstrate.

Dolphin

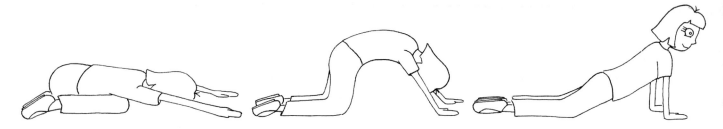

Knees and feet should be together.

The teacher says to the children:

"Smoothly move your body forward through the three positions and backwards by reversing the sequence. This should be a smooth, continuous motion. Slowly move your body back and forth as if you are a dolphin gliding through the ocean."

The teacher shows the illustrations for the **Rainbow** pose for the children to learn and demonstrate.

Rainbow	**Rainbow (Variation #1)** **More Difficult**	**Rainbow (Variation #2)** **Most Difficult**

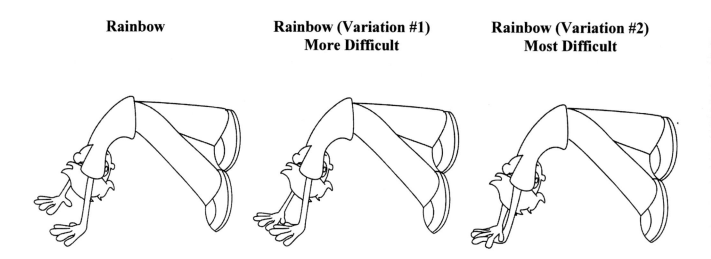

Discuss the story and its meaning.

Suggestions:

- Read various excerpts from the story for the children to explain its meaning.
- When you close your eyes and visualize yourself, what kind of a person do you see? Or whom do you see? Describe yourself.
- Name some things that make you feel good about yourself or proud of yourself.
- What kind of positive things do you visualize yourself doing?
- How can you use visualization and positive thoughts to accomplish your goals?
- What does quest mean?
- How can self-control and focus help you accomplish your goals?
- Why is it important to have a positive attitude?
- Why is it important to say positive things to yourself?
- What does it mean to persevere?
- What does endurance mean?
- Why is it important to believe in yourself?
- How do you feel when your body is calm and resting?
- Why is it important to calm your thoughts and your body before you make a choice?
- Read an excerpt from the story for the children to visualize and draw a picture of the words they hear.

Tell the children to get into the **Relax** pose. Add background music (optional). The teacher says, "Close your eyes and visualize yourself doing things that encourage happiness in yourself. What makes you feel happy?"

After the children have been given a few minutes to rest in the **Relax** pose, tell them to complete the following sentences:

- I love to ………
- I will work hard to be better at……….

<u>Activity #52:</u> <u>The Gift of Peace</u>

<u>Suggested Reading (optional):</u>

- What Does Peace Feel Like? By V. Radunsk
- Peace Begins With You by Katherine Scholes

<u>Directions:</u>

The teacher reads the following story, *The Gift of Peace*. Tell the children to focus (pay attention/concentrate) on the words they hear.

The teacher tells the children to visualize what the story looks like in their imaginations.

The Gift of Peace

What do you see in the sky at night? I see shooting stars, twinkling lights, and moonbeams flashing across the sky in sight.

Moonbeams are filled with special gifts — sending streams of shimmering colors filled with sparkling lights as they dash across the sky in flight.

Moonbeams dance and spin around — calm and peaceful — with a magical sound.

Big and tall, short and small, dark and light — so many colors, shapes, and heights. Some are narrow, some are wide, but all these differences are pushed aside — and with strength and courage across the universe, moonbeams glide — planting virtue in your spirit, heart, and soul. Peace and harmony — the ultimate goal!

Moonbeam, Moonbeam, where do you hide? Come and dance by my side.

A vision of peace so magnificent to see; I will keep it here inside of me.
And through this verse of dance and song, I promise to pass this vision along.

A silvery stream of sparkling light danced around my body that night.
The moonbeam waltzed around so free — leaving with me a special key.

This magnificent key that you receive brings a special gift — *to always believe.*
Believe in yourself and you will feel the courage, strength, and unity to make this vision reality.

I promise to unlock the spirit in me with this very special key — filled with strength and courage and peace and hope — what a difference I can make with this gift I promise to take.

From dawn to dusk, the small child danced, but, once she passed the key along, there were two, three, four, and more children dancing through the streets. You could hear the tapping of their feet.

Big and tall, short and small, dark and light — so many colors, shapes, and heights. Some are narrow, some are wide, but all these differences are pushed aside — and with strength and courage across the universe, they glide — spreading peace and strength and unity as they sing "I believe in you and me."

Peace and hope and harmony — I will always keep inside of me and share with you this special key, a symbol of peace that was given to me.

I will unlock the peace inside of me, and through this verse of dance and song, I promise to pass this key along.

A vision of peace so magnificent to see — I will pass it along to you from me. Planting virtue in your spirit, heart, and soul — peace and harmony — the ultimate goal!

Discuss the story and its meaning.

Suggestions:

- Where does peace begin? (Within yourself). Why?
- What is the key a symbol of? (Peace).
- Why does the key represent peace? (It unlocks the peace inside of you).
- What happens when you unlock the peace inside of you? (You can give peace to others to pass along).
- What is virtue? (Goodness).
- Name some different ways that you can show peace.
- Name some different ways that you can show strength and courage.
- How can you pass peace along to others?
- What is a moonbeam?
- Describe a moonbeam.
- What are moonbeams filled with?

Exercise #1:

Directions:

Tell the children to draw a picture of their vision of peace. A vision is what you see in your imagination, creating your own thoughts and ideas.

Draw a picture of:

Your vision of peace or what does peace look like to you?

Select calm and quiet background music (optional) and encourage the children to draw their peaceful thoughts and ideas.

Other Suggestions:

- Have the children cut out a picture of a key and color it. They can also wear their keys to represent peace.
- Have the children create peaceful movements to music or create their own dance of peace.
- Create a peace collage with pictures cut from magazines that represent peace.
- Choose an excerpt from the story, *The Gift of Peace*. Read the passage for the children to visualize and draw a picture of the words they hear.

Exercise #2:

Materials Needed:

- Peace Jar
- Marbles or Paper Clips

Directions:

- Set aside a day designated for Peace Day or an entire week for Peace Week. Tell the children they are going to create a Peace Movement by giving peace (sharing, using velvet words, being considerate, resolving conflicts peacefully, etc.) to others. Explain to the children that they have to show peace within themselves so that they can pass their peaceful ways along to others (like the moonbeams in the story, *The Gift of Peace*).

- Tell the children their Peace Movement begins by going on a peace hunt. They are going to look for peace throughout their school (in the classroom, on the playground, in the halls, etc.) by observing the actions of others. Each time a child observes peace somewhere in their school, they describe what peaceful action they saw and where they saw it. All teachers throughout the school should participate in this activity. This gives children the opportunity to observe their friends and teachers demonstrating peace and giving peace to others.

- Each time a child or teacher observes peace they place a marble or a paper clip to represent the peaceful action in their peace jar. At the end of the week discuss their Peace Movement (giving peace to others) and count (the marbles or paper clips) how many peaceful actions they observed.

- Placing marbles or paper clips in their peace jar inspires the children to create a visual image of peace. For example, this marble represents sharing, caring, thoughtfulness, being calm, or patience.

- Reward children by using positive language and positive reinforcement, such as, *you should feel proud of yourselves, you passed along so many peaceful thoughts and actions to others and also recognized peaceful actions in others.* Discuss specific peaceful actions the children observed, such as, *that was really thoughtful to let Rachel go first.* Encourage the children to tell themselves *I did a good job or it feels good to help others.*

Teaching Tip:

This activity inspires children to choose positive behavior based on their conscience, not a reward. It gives children the opportunity to practice peace within themselves and share peace with others. This activity encourages children to visualize and practice peace: *I know what peace looks like. I know what peace feels like.*

Exercise #3:

Directions:

Discuss with the children the following concepts:

- Self-Control.
- Focus.
- Positive/Negative Consequences.
- Peace & Hope.
- Strength & Courage.
- Emotional/Mental & Physical Strength.
- Velvet & Sandpaper Words/Actions.
- Self-Talk.
- Positive Thoughts.
- Visualization.
- Feelings.

- Confidence.
- Why is it important to control your actions?
- How to create a Peace Movement.
- Perseverance.
- Organizing your thoughts (ideas) & your body (actions).
- I feel good about myself when I help others.
- Believing in yourself.
- Visualizing peace.

Exercise #4:

Materials Needed:

- Copy and print the illustrations of the following **Peace** poses for the children to learn and demonstrate. You may have already printed these poses from activity #9, peace.

Directions:

The teacher says to the children, "Let's all sit in the **Peace** pose."

- Take a deep breath.
- Visualize your STAR.
- Say to yourself: *I am a STAR!*
- When you visualize your STAR and say to yourself, *I am a STAR*, what does it remind you to do?
- How does being a STAR create peace?
- Recite the Peace Pledge (p. 74).

Discuss with the children how they can create peace in their school, in their classrooms, in their homes, and in the community.

The teacher and the children demonstrate the **Peace** sequence together.

Peace

Circle of Peace

Giving Peace

Poses and Moving Balances

Quiet & Still (sitting)

Quiet & Still (standing)

Peace

Circle of Peace

Giving Peace

Relax

Bow & Arrow

Bridge

Tricycle

Bicycle

Relaxing Star

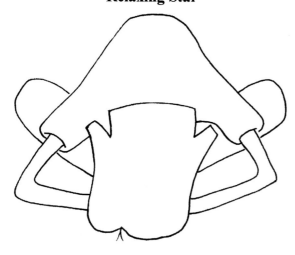

- Sitting with legs crisscrossed.

Twinkling Star

- Gently and slowly wiggle your fingers and shoulders.
- Concentrate on keeping your lower body still.

Rising Star

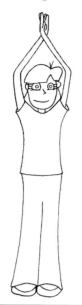

Put Your Body Back Together

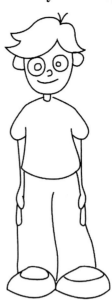

Elevator Up

Elevator Down

- Lift your knees (legs stay criss-crossed) and place your feet flat on the floor.
- Rock your body forward and roll on to your feet (hands stay on your head). Smoothly and slowly rise to a standing position (knees slightly bent).

- Slowly and smoothly lower your body to the floor (keeping your hands on your head) to a sitting position (legs remain criss-crossed).

Turtle/Tortoise

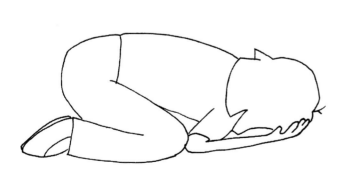

Tilt

Reaching

- Balance on your opposite hand and foot.
- Focus on the floor.
- Hold for a few seconds, then change to your other hand and foot.

Ankle Balance

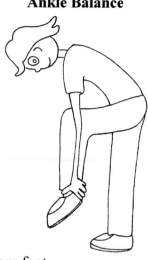

- Focus on your foot.
- Hold for a few seconds, change and hold on to your other ankle and balance.

Ankle Balance: (more difficult)

Lift

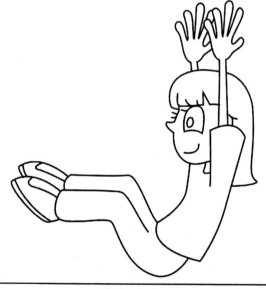

"L"

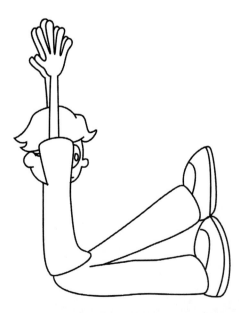

Sideways

Kitty Cat Stretch

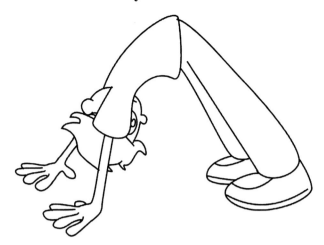

Table-Top Tummy

Reaching for the Stars

Dolphin - 1

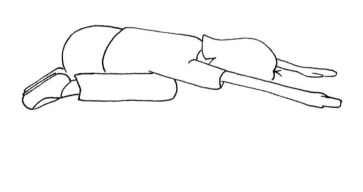

Dolphin - 2

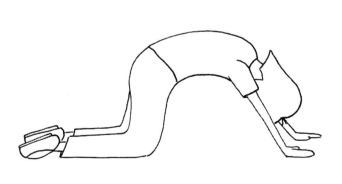

Dolphin - 3

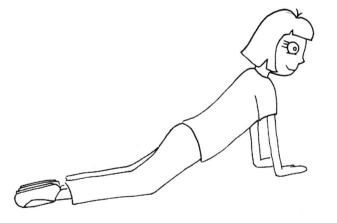

Rainbow

**Rainbow
(variation #1 - more difficult)**

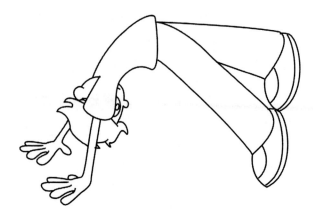 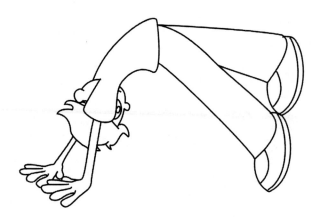

**Rainbow
(variation #2 - most difficult)**

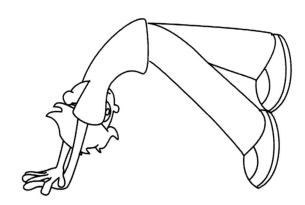

Cooperation Poses

Mountain

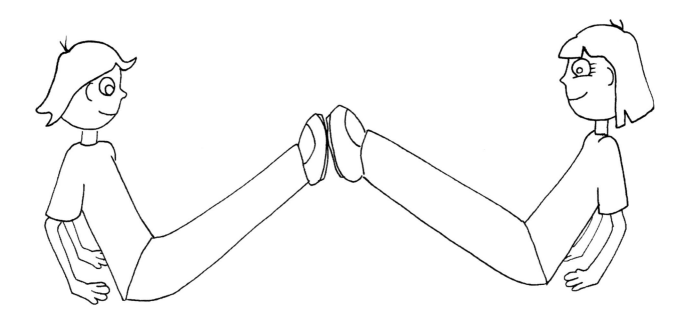

Canoeing

- Children coordinate their bodies with each other by leaning forward and backward at the same time.
- Children lean forward with straight arms.
- Children lean back while bending their elbows.
- This should be a quiet, smooth, and continuous movement as if rowing a boat.
- This movement can be done with two or more children.

Bridge

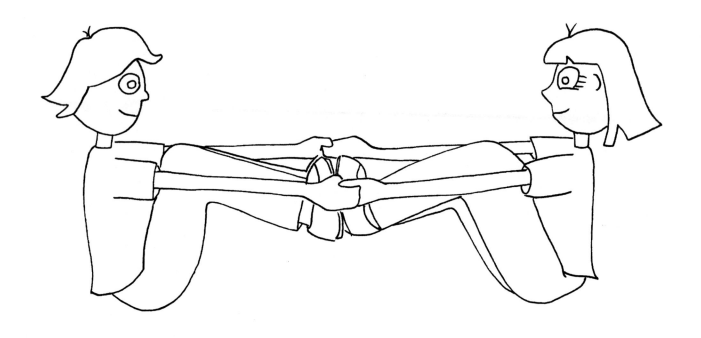

Bicycle Built For Two

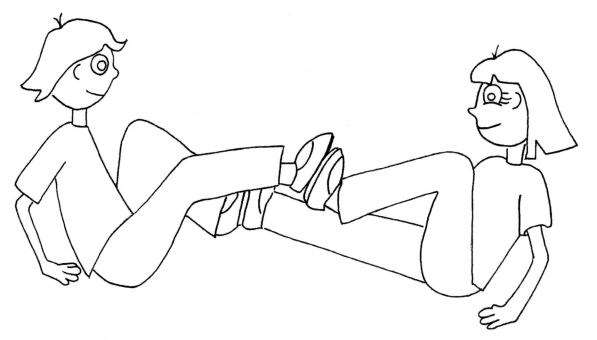

• Children coordinate their bodies with each other by moving their feet back and forth as if pedaling a bicycle.

Suggested Reading: Learn Important Concepts and Skills Through Literature

Add additional fun to storytime by encouraging children to participate in the story by asking questions such as, *what do you think will happen next? How do you think this story will end? Or let's think of some different ways you could handle this situation.*

In familiar stories leave out the end of certain sentences in the story and let your child complete them.

- On Monday When It Rained by Cherryl Kachenmeister
- Anh's Anger by Gail Silver
- Steps and Stones by Gail Silver
- I Believe by Jamie Goldring
- How to be a Friend by Laurie Krasny and Marc Brown
- Sometimes I Feel Like a Mouse by Jeanne Modesitt
- Walther Was Worried by Laura Vaccaro Seeger
- The Happiest Tree, a Yoga Story by Uma Krishnaswami
- The First Forest by John Gile
- I Like Me! By Nancy Carlson
- How Do I Feel? By Norma Simon
- I Was So Mad! By Norma Simon
- Will I Have a Friend? By Miriam Cohen
- All Kinds of Children by Norma Simon
- A to Z Do You Ever Feel Like Me? By Bonnie Hausman
- Sometimes I'm Bombaloo by Rachel Vail
- I Am a Good Citizen by Mary Ann Hoffman
- Peacefulness by Lucia Raatma
- Peacefulness by Ralene Diaco
- Peacefulness by Rebecca Olien
- Who Am I? by Suzanne Mulcahy
- Mean Soup by Betsy Everitt
- Chrysanthemum by Kevin Henkes
- Giving by Shirley Hughes
- Be A Frog, A Bird, or A Tree by Rachel Carr
- I'm Gonna Like Me by Jamie Lee Curtis
- Words Are Not For Hurting by Elizabeth Verdick
- Teasing Trouble by Valerie Tripp
- Hunter's Best Friend at School by Laura Malone Elliott
- Spaghetti in a Hot Dog Bun by Maria Dismondy
- Have You Filled a Bucket Today? By Carol Mc Cloud
- Odd Velvet by Mary E. Whitcomb
- Stand Tall, Molly Lou Melon by Patty Lovel
- We Can Work it Out by Barbara K. Polland
- Ready, Set, Swim! By Gail Donovan
- Being Careless by Joy Berry
- Being Bossy by Joy Berry
- Whining by Joy Berry
- Teasing By Joy Berry
- Being Selfish by Joy Berry
- Frustrated by Sylvia Root Tester
- Zach Gets Frustrated by William Mulcahy
- Dealing with Arguments by Lisa K. Adams
- Dealing with Teasing by Lisa K.Adams
- Dealing with Anger by Marianne Johnston
- All My Feelings At Home by Susan Conlin & Susan Levine Friedman
- Feeling Scared by Helen Frost
- Thoughts & Feelings; Afraid by Susan Riley
- Thoughts & Feelings; Sharing by Susan Riley
- Thoughts & Feelings; Angry by Susan Riley
- Thoughts & Feelings; Success by Susan Riley

- Thoughts & Feelings; I'm Sorry by Susan Riley
- Thoughts & Feelings; Help by Susan Riley
- Thoughts & Feelings; Glad by Elizabeth Budd
- When I Feel Scared by Cornelia Maude Spelman
- The Great Big Book of Families by Mary Hoffman
- The Giving Tree by Shel Silverstein
- The Missing Piece by Shel Silverstein
- Chicken Soup for Little Souls: The Goodness Gorillas by Lisa McCourt
- Let's Talk About Feeling Lonely by Melanie Ann Apel
- Let's Talk About When You Think Nobody Likes You by Melanie Ann Apel
- Let's Talk About Feeling Confused by Melanie Ann Apel
- Let's Talk About Feeling Worried by Melanie Ann Apel
- Let's Talk About Feeling Defeated by Melanie Ann Apel
- Let's Talk About Nightmares by Melanie Ann Apel
- When I'm Angry by Jane Aaron
- The Day Leo Said I Hate You! By Robie H. Harris
- I'm So Mad by Robie H. Harris
- Being Angry by Julie Johnson
- When Sophie Gets Angry—Really, Really Angry by Molly Bang
- The Hating Book by Charlotte Zolotow
- Franklin is Bossy by Paulette Bourgeois
- Amazing Grace by Mary Hoffman
- How to Loose All Your Friends by Nancy Carlson
- Mimi the Selfish Kitten by Time-Life Editors
- Be Nice by Kate Tym
- D. W. The Big Boss by Marc Brown
- Bullies Are a Pain in the Brain by Trevor Romain
- How to Take the GRRRR Out of Anger by Elizabeth Verdick and Marjorie Lisovskis
- How to Handle Bullies, Teasers, and Other Meanies by Kate Cohen-Posey
- Chester's Way by Kevin Henkes
- Enemy Pie by Derek Munson
- Crazy Hair Day by Barney Saltzberg
- Horace and Morris but Mostly Dolores by James Howe
- Alexander and the Terrible, Horrible, No Good, Very Bad Day
- The Rainbow Fish by Marcus Pfister
- I Am a Leader by Sarah L. Schuette
- The Ball, The Book, and The Drum by Morgan Troll
- I'm Not Happy by Sue Graves
- But why Can't I by Sue Graves
- Best Friends by Steven Kellogg
- All I See by Cynthia Rylant
- My Best Friend by Pat Hutchins
- My Friend Rabbit by Eric Rohmann
- Two Cool Coyotes by Jillian Lund
- Polly's Picnic by Richard Hamilton
- Music, Music For Everyone by Vera B. Williams
- I Feel Lonely by Katie Kawa
- I Feel Angry by Kelly Doudna
- I Feel Happy by Kelly Doudna
- I Feel Sad by Kellly Doudna
- I Feel Safe by Kelly Doudna
- I Feel Scared by Kelly Doudna
- I Will Be Especially Very Careful by Lauren Child
- Looking After Myself by Sarah Levete
- Making Friends by Sarah Levete